# Unlocking the Strategic Use of Public Procurement in Bratislava, Slovak Republic

OECD

BETTER POLICIES FOR BETTER LIVES

This document, as well as any data and map included herein, are without prejudice to the status of or sovereignty over any territory, to the delimitation of international frontiers and boundaries and to the name of any territory, city or area.

**Please cite this publication as:**
OECD (2021), *Unlocking the Strategic Use of Public Procurement in Bratislava, Slovak Republic*, OECD Publishing, Paris, *https://doi.org/10.1787/d616e4d9-en*.

ISBN 978-92-64-77960-0 (print)
ISBN 978-92-64-70798-6 (pdf)

# Foreword

Across OECD countries, public procurement of goods, services and infrastructures accounts for around 12% of gross domestic product (GDP), playing an important role in driving smart, sustainable and inclusive growth, including supporting the recovery from the COVID-19 pandemic. Subnational governments, including cities, carry out over 60% of total public procurement in OECD countries.

Based on acquired evidence and international best practices in OECD member and partner countries, this report summarises the outcomes from a 17-month long policy dialogue between the OECD and the city of Bratislava. It provides cross-cutting analysis and policy recommendations on the drivers, bottlenecks and opportunities for the city's strategic use of public procurement. The report includes a specific focus on the design of the procurement strategy of Bratislava's street lighting system and provides methodological guidance on the analysis of needs, market engagement and tender design.

This report underlines that public procurement offers a strategic tool for cities not only to serve the needs of citizens but also to boost innovation, competitiveness, productivity and resilience, drive an inclusive recovery and support the transition to a low-carbon economy. The tailored findings and policy recommendations for Bratislava can inspire other cities to adopt more efficient procurement processes, engage more closely with industry for purchasing innovative and sustainable solutions, and strive for greater efficiency in national public procurement systems.

The final report was approved via written procedure by the Regional Development Policy Committee (RDPC) and the Public Governance Committee (PGC) on 4 November 2021 under the cote COM/CFE/RDPC/GOV/PGC(2021)3.

# Acknowledgements

This report was prepared jointly by the OECD Centre for Entrepreneurship, SMEs, Regions and Cities (CFE) led by Lamia Kamal-Chaoui, Director, and the OECD Directorate for Public Governance (GOV) led by Elsa Pilichowski, Director, as part of the Programme of Work and Budget of the OECD Regional Development Policy Committee (RDPC) and the OECD Public Governance Committee (PGC). It results from a policy dialogue with key stakeholders from public, private and non-profit sectors across all levels of government in Bratislava, Slovak Republic.

The report was drafted by a core team of OECD policy analysts comprised of Kenza Khachani (GOV) and Aline Matta (CFE), co-ordinated by Soo-Jin Kim, Deputy Head of the Cities, Urban Policies and Sustainable Development Division (CFE), and Paulo Magina, Deputy Head of the Infrastructure and Public Procurement Division (GOV), under the supervision of Aziza Akhmouch, Head of the Cities, Urban Policies and Sustainable Development Division (CFE), and Edwin Lau, Head of the Infrastructure and Public Procurement Division (GOV).

The report also benefitted from valuable input from Erika Bozzay (GOV), Eric Gonnard (CFE), Stefano Marta (CFE) and Miroslava Packova (GOV).

The OECD Secretariat is grateful for the high-level political impetus and commitment from Mr Matus Vallo, Mayor of Bratislava. Special thanks are conveyed to the local team in Bratislava, composed of Eduard Donauer, Michal Garaj and Juraj Nyulassy, for their excellent collaboration with the OECD and their professionalism. The OECD Secretariat would also like to thank the different stakeholders interviewed in the framework of this review and that provided relevant input.

Thanks are extended to François Iglesias and Pilar Philip (CFE), Elisabetta Pilati and Lauren Thwaites (GOV) for preparing the report for publication, and to Eleonore Morena for editing and formatting it.

# Table of contents

## Tables

## Figures

## Boxes

## Follow OECD Publications on:

http://twitter.com/OECD_Pubs

http://www.facebook.com/OECDPublications

http://www.linkedin.com/groups/OECD-Publications-4645871

http://www.youtube.com/oecdilibrary

http://www.oecd.org/oecddirect/

# Abbreviations and acronyms

| | |
|---|---|
| BPQR | Best price quality ratio |
| CA | Contracting authority |
| CMS | Control and management system |
| COVID-19 | Coronavirus Disease 2019 |
| DPS | Dynamic purchasing systems |
| EO | Economic operators |
| EU | European Union |
| FA | Framework agreement |
| FUA | Functional urban area |
| GDP | Gross domestic product |
| GPP | Green public procurement |
| HPS | High-pressure sodium |
| ICT | Information and communication technology |
| IoT | Internet of Things |
| ITI | Integrated territorial investment |
| KPI | Key performance indicator |
| LCC | Life cycle costing |
| LED | Light-emitting diode |
| LTE | Long-Term Evolution |
| NGO | Non-governmental organisation |
| PD | Procurement department |
| PIN | Prior information notice |
| PPA | Public Procurement Act |
| PPO | Public Procurement Office |
| RfP | Request for proposal |
| RfQ | Request for quotation |
| SDG | United Nations Sustainable Development Goal |
| SMART | Specific, Measurable, Assignable, Realistic and Time-related |
| SME | Small- and medium-sized enterprise |

# Executive summary

Public procurement can offer a powerful tool to stimulate innovation, facilitate the transition to a green and circular economy, support small- and medium-sized enterprises (SMEs) and promote ethical behaviour and responsible business conduct. In addition, in many cities, the COVID-19 pandemic further increased pressure on local spending and public procurement procedures. This report aims at supporting the city of Bratislava in its efforts to make procurement a catalyst for change in identifying better value-for-money solutions, fostering competition and ensuring sustainable urban development. The report is particularly timely as the city is currently preparing new directives on public procurement, which represent promising steps to enhance its public procurement system. The report also includes a case study on street lighting to support the city in designing the most adequate procurement strategies for improving the quality and expected outcomes of its future integrated system.

## Key findings

### Drivers and barriers to make Bratislava smarter, greener and more inclusive through public procurement

- In 2019, while public procurement represented 20.6% of subnational government expenditure in the Slovak Republic, it accounted for 39% (EUR 145 million) of Bratislava's expenditure.
- The COVID-19 crisis called for reinforcing the need to streamline and improve the procurement system of Bratislava to advance its strategic priorities.
- Although Bratislava has developed new internal directives to reform its procurement processes, it has not yet exploited the full potential to guide urban policy and use the United Nations' Sustainable Development Goals (SDGs) as a reference framework. For example, neither the latest city strategy (2010-20) nor the draft of the forthcoming one explicitly address the role of public procurement in achieving the city's objectives.
- Even though public procurement generally involves using taxpayers' money, consultation of citizens about their needs has remained limited so far in Bratislava. For instance, the city has not implemented any participatory budgeting processes.

### Using public procurement strategically in the city of Bratislava

- Faced with the urgent need to purchase essential goods in the early stage of the COVID-19 pandemic, Bratislava fast-tracked its procurement process by removing some steps. Nonetheless, the system for approval and workflows remains mainly paper-based and the city does not have a central database for contracts or documents such as market analysis, which would help consolidate the information in one place and accelerate procedures.
- Effective needs analysis requires identifying the needs of end users in terms of performance, functionalities, quality and quantity of the necessary solution. On average, only 40% of approved

procurement plans in Bratislava have been executed. While the disruption caused by the COVID-19 pandemic may explain part of this low rate of execution in 2020, other pre-existing barriers relate, for instance, to the lack of capacity to undertake needs analysis.

- When undertaking needs analysis, Bratislava's approach tends to focus on products and services already available on the market rather than solutions and functions.

- The public procurement system in Bratislava is mostly decentralised, as the 44 organisations belonging to the city, such as the waste management company and the transport company, conduct their own procurement. Although their needs are sometimes aggregated and presented jointly to the market, there is no clear methodology to inform decisions on the potential aggregation of needs.

- Although Bratislava has used preliminary market consultation for a few tenders, no clear guidance is provided to the city officials on the methods to engage the market.

- Even though the vast majority of tenders were launched via a competitive process, the most frequently used methodology to assess tenders is still based on the lowest price rather than encompassing a variety of criteria, which would help promote broader objectives such as innovation and sustainability.

- Bratislava has started to leverage the benefits of collaborative procurement instruments by implementing eight framework agreements and four dynamic purchasing systems (DPS). However, no comprehensive data is available to assess the amounts spent in each procurement category and identify where collaborative procurement could help further increase efficiency.

- SMEs in Bratislava are not reaping the full benefit of public procurement yet. Between April 2016 and May 2020, 69% of procedures were awarded to SMEs but this represented less than half of the total procurement volume (40%).

- Bratislava does not undertake any regular evaluation to assess existing procurement processes. However, the city is aiming at implementing relevant key performance indicators (KPIs).

- While public procurement data of the city of Bratislava is available from different sources, they do not allow citizens and stakeholders to explore the data in a user-friendly format following the budget cycle.

- Several city departments conduct procurement activities but they often lack adequate technical capacity. Indeed, no capacity-building activities on procurement are available to those officials.

- Bratislava has no formal risk management assessment on procurement activities to inform its strategies. However, risks may be discussed at the individual procurement level.

## Policy recommendations

To unlock the potential of public procurement to drive more inclusive, smart and sustainable growth, the city of Bratislava could:

- Make the strategic role of public procurement explicit in the new city strategy (2021-30).

- Leverage procurement as a tool to achieve the SDGs and reflect SDG-related mechanisms in the new internal public procurement directives.

- Analyse the relevance of integrating advance payments in the new internal public procurement directives and further promote allotment strategies to support SME development.

- Use strategically public procurement to advance the innovation agenda of the city.

- Map the stakeholders involved in procurement activities and put in place a more effective cross-cutting organisational structure to co-ordinate procurement processes among city departments.

- Make its portal interactive to better understand the needs of citizens and involve them upstream in consultations to shape procurement processes, including in participatory budgeting processes.
- Continue its efforts to streamline the procurement processes in the new internal public procurement directives and further digitalise procurement processes.
- Develop specific KPIs to monitor and evaluate procurement outcomes. In this regard, the city could consider not only refining its internal system to collect relevant procurement data but also making the data transparent and accessible.
- Provide guidance to city departments on the methods to engage the market and collect information, and consider developing a market analysis template.
- Analyse the procurement spending plans of each municipal organisation of the city to identify opportunities for aggregating needs or using collaborative procurement instruments, including framework agreements and DPS.
- Further use the best price quality ratio (BPQR) criteria to enable contracting authorities to assess bids not only on the basis of price but also on other aspects.
- Identify key competencies for city officials involved in procurement operations and develop tailored training programmes on procurement processes and mechanisms.
- Enhance the capacity of city officials in different public procurement processes and activities.
- Provide procurement stakeholders with data on procurement spending in a harmonised, user-friendly format.
- Put in place a comprehensive risk management strategy for its procurement operations.

## Case study on public procurement for street lighting in Bratislava

### Overview of the current street lighting system in Bratislava

- Many parts of the current street lighting system in Bratislava are outdated and require urgent investments. Bratislava has therefore started an ambitious project to improve security, achieve energy efficiency, reduce maintenance costs, ensure better data management and generate revenue. The goal is to have public lighting fully covered with smart light-emitting diodes (LEDs) within 5 years (by 2025), with estimated savings of more than 40% in total energy consumption.
- Instead of awarding one contract to an economic operator to operate and maintain the street lighting system, the city decided to split the investment into several contracts with several providers. In addition, given the budget constraints and the three-year limitation on Bratislava's multi-year budgeting, many of the procurement activities necessary to renew the street lighting system cannot be planned yet.

### Ways forward on public procurement for street lighting in Bratislava

1. Undertake thorough market analysis for each street lighting component by leveraging pilot projects (such as the public procurement of park lighting) to improve upcoming tender documentation and publish a prior information notice when relevant to positively impact competition.
2. Reinforce citizen engagement in the street lighting project through meetings or by using digital tools.
3. Use a life cycle approach when assessing bids and increase the weight of the qualitative and other non-price criteria to enhance value-for-money outcomes.
4. Further explore the benefits of DPS in the framework of the street lighting project.

# 1. Drivers and barriers to public procurement in Bratislava

This chapter depicts Bratislava's territorial and economic profile through a snapshot of its territorial organisation, demography and economic trends. It reviews the city's role in providing public services and provides an overview of the institutional and regulatory public procurement framework in the city. It also looks at the role of citizens in budgetary and procurement choices for better services. The chapter concludes with a call for rethinking the role of public procurement in the city's new strategic vision.

## 1.1. Bratislava's territorial and economic profile

### 1.1.1. Snapshot of Bratislava's territorial organisation, demography and economic trends

The city of Bratislava is the capital of the Slovak Republic. Bratislava is divided administratively into 17 boroughs within five districts: Bratislava I (city centre), Bratislava II (eastern sector), Bratislava III (northeastern sector), Bratislava IV (western and northern sectors) and Bratislava V (southern sector). As of 2020, Bratislava's population counts 437 726 inhabitants (Statistical Office of the Slovak Republic, 2021[1]). Bratislava is the highest populated city in the Slovak Republic when considering its functional urban area (FUA), as reported in 2019 (Eurostat, 2021[2]). In 2017, for instance, the city counted approximately 140 000 daily commuters (OECD, 2020[3]).

The FUA of Bratislava is composed of the core city (hereinafter called "the city") and less densely populated local units that surround it and are part of the city's labour market (called "commuting zone"). As described in Figure 1.1, in 2019 the metropolitan area of Bratislava itself was home to 12% of the national population (Eurostat, 2021[2]). The concept of an FUA can guide city governments in their procurement decisions when they plan infrastructure, for example, when it comes to transportation, housing, schools and cultural and recreational spaces. Co-ordination across municipal boundaries, including on public investment and public procurement, is critical because decisions in one municipality can have consequences for outcomes in other municipalities (OECD, forthcoming[4]). Strong co-operation is therefore required between the city of Bratislava, surrounding municipalities and the regional and national levels, to provide better services to citizens and businesses, which will be discussed in the following sections.

**Figure 1.1. Population of the FUAs in the Slovak Republic, 2019**

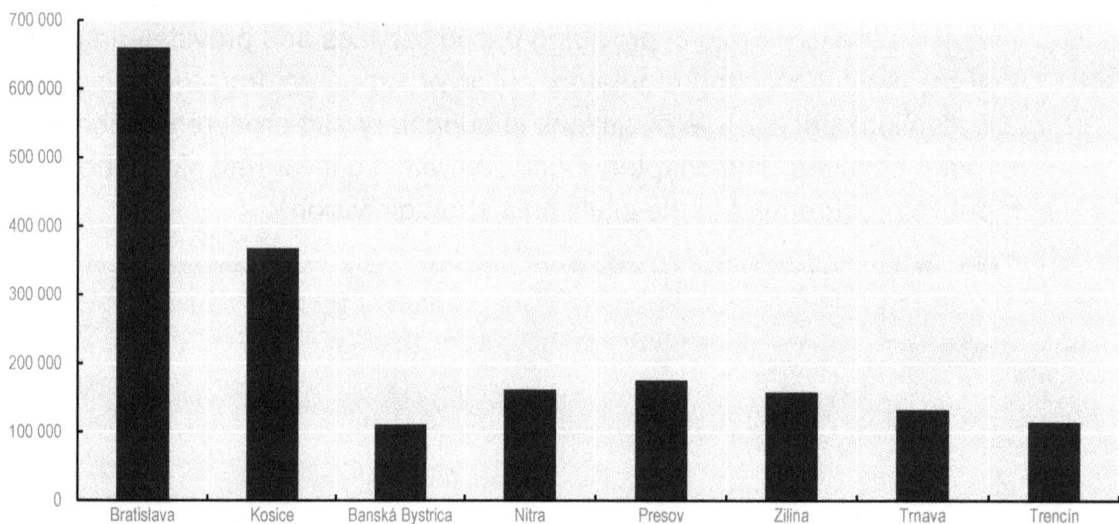

Source: Eurostat (2021[5]), *Population on 1 January by Age Groups and Sex - Functional Urban Areas*, http://appsso.eurostat.ec.europa.eu/nui/show.do?dataset=urb_lpop1&lang=en.

The metropolitan area of Bratislava accounts for 19% of the national gross domestic product (GDP) in 2018. Between 2000 and 2018, it generated 21% of the national GDP growth. Bratislava is among the top third metropolitan areas in the OECD in terms of GDP per capita, ranking 130 out of 490 metropolitan areas in 2018 (OECD.Stat, 2021[6]). GDP per capita in Bratislava is above the average of OECD metropolitan areas, lower than in Prague (Czech Republic) and Vienna (Austria) metropolitan areas but higher than in Budapest (Hungary). With a GDP per capita value that is 60% higher than that of the country,

Bratislava is among the richest capital metropolitan areas in the OECD, relative to the overall country. The city ranks among the top 28% of OECD metropolitan areas of more than 250 000 inhabitants in terms of GDP per capita growth since 2000 (OECD, 2020[3]). GDP per capita has increased by 1.7% per year between 2001 and 2018 (OECD, 2020[3]) (Figure 1.2).

## Figure 1.2. Trends in GDP per capita in Bratislava and selected metropolitan areas, 2018

FUAs above 500 000 people, Slovak Republic and surrounding OECD countries

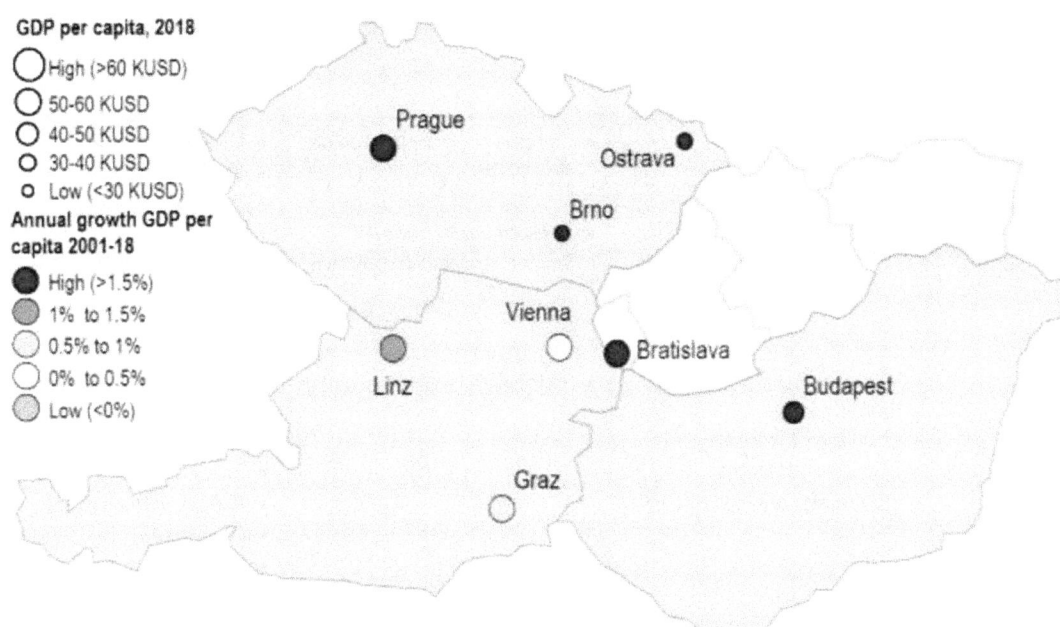

Source: OECD.Stat (2021[6]), *OECD Metropolitan (database)*, https://stats.oecd.org/Index.aspx?Datasetcode=CITIES.

### *1.1.2. The key role of Bratislava in the provision of public services*

Decentralisation reforms introduced in 2001-02 and throughout 2005 in the Slovak Republic increased the competencies and resources of its subnational governments, including municipalities. Municipalities have significant responsibilities and competencies in urban planning and local public services such as social assistance, housing, environment, primary schools and recreation. Their responsibilities are divided between own competencies and competencies devolved by the central government. Table 1.1 lists services provided by the central government, regions and municipalities. The Slovak Republic has a decentralised governance system based on a two-tier system of subnational government. The status of "city" is granted by the parliament to municipalities that are an administrative, economic and cultural centre providing public services to neighbouring municipalities. These "cities" have, however, the same responsibilities as other municipalities.

The municipal level (2 927 municipalities) includes cities (*mesto*) (141 municipalities), rural municipalities (2 744 municipalities), city districts in Bratislava (17 districts) and Košice (22 districts), as well as 3 military districts (OECD/UCLG, 2016[7]; Statistical Office of Slovak Republic, 2021[8]). City districts in the cities of Bratislava and Košice also have a "municipality" status (although they are contained within a municipality) and are responsible for issues such as urban planning, local road maintenance and ordinances, budget, park maintenance and public safety (OECD/UCLG, 2019[9]). Within this broader distribution of responsibilities, each level of government is responsible for its own procurement operations to fulfil its responsibilities. There is therefore a need to have a capable procurement workforce at all levels of governments, including at the local level.

**Table 1.1. The main responsibilities of national and subnational governments in the Slovak Republic**

| Responsibilities | National level | Regional level | Municipal level |
|---|---|---|---|
| General public services | • Internal administration International co-operation | • Internal administration International and trans-regional co-operation | • Internal administration<br>• Management of movable property and real estate owned by the municipality, or transferred temporarily by the state<br>• Building permits<br>• Registry offices |
| Public order and safety | | • Civil defence (in co-operation with state bodies) | • Municipal police<br>• Public order<br>• Firefighting |
| Economic affairs/ transport | • Transport (roads, railways, inland waterways) | • Transport (roads, railways)<br>• Regional economic development | • Supervision of economic activities<br>• Consumer protection<br>• Local roads<br>• Local public transport<br>• Tourism |
| Environmental protection | • National environmental policy<br>• National parks<br>• Environmental monitoring<br>• Environmental burdens | • Environmental educational centres | • Protection of the environment<br>• Sewerage<br>• Heating<br>• Refuse collection and disposal |
| Housing and community amenities | • State housing development fund | | • Housing and town planning<br>• Cemeteries<br>• Public lightning<br>• Water supply<br>• Parks and open spaces<br>• Urban regeneration<br>• Social housing |
| Health | • National health policy<br>• Hospitals (teaching hospitals) | • Secondary hospitals<br>• Management of non-state healthcare such as psychiatric hospitals and dental services | • First aid stations and primary medical centres |
| Recreation, culture and religion | • National cultural facilities (galleries/theatre)<br>• Cultural subsidies | • Regional theatres<br>• Libraries<br>• Museums<br>• Galleries<br>• Cultural centres | • Sports facilities<br>• Cultural facilities |
| Education | • Tertiary education<br>• Financial transfers for secondary and primary education | • Secondary, professional, art and vocational schools<br>• Construction and maintenance of buildings<br>• Payment of teachers on behalf of the state | • Pre-school and primary schools<br>• Kindergarten and nurseries |
| Social protection | • National social policy<br>• National projects – European Union (EU) funding of social fieldwork | • Homes for children | • Social aid for elderly and children |

Source: OECD/UCLG (2019[9]), *2019 Report of the World Observatory on Subnational Government Finance and Investment – Country Profiles*, https://www.sng-wofi.org/publications/SNGWOFI_2019_report_country_profiles.pdf; answers from the city of Bratislava to the OECD questionnaire and during the OECD fact-finding mission in February 2021.

*Transport services*

The provision of public transport is one of the most prioritised policy areas in Bratislava. The public transport network in the city is the largest in the Slovak Republic. The transport system plays a critical role in making parts of the city viable places to build homes and create jobs (OECD, 2020[10]) and to provide access to residents commuting into the city from the surrounding areas (commuting flows). Although the city aims to improve the experience of public transport users, it still faces three main challenges to extend its network and improve mobility. The first challenge relates to the expansion of the tram network, which was put to a halt in the 1980s as Bratislava started to build a metro line but suspended its construction due to feasibility challenges. The second challenge is the lack of capacity of the transport market. According to Bratislava, there are only two engineering companies capable of working on tram extension in the Slovak Republic. They have not been sufficient to absorb the work in Bratislava due to their size and the resources available. The third challenge is a lack of budget, which could result in unfinished infrastructure projects. The procurement volume related to public transport and mobility accounted for around EUR 79 million in 2020. Bratislava is planning an additional EUR 75 million of procurement for the tram line in 2021. However, the transport infrastructure is mainly financed by EU funding, while maintenance is financed by tax revenues generated by the city transport company. To advance procurement processes, the city's department of transport, which is mainly in charge of developing policies, setting priorities and securing infrastructure (e.g. bus stops), could work closely with the city-owned company (*Dopravný podnik Bratislava*), which is in charge of the transport system and provides three types of transport services (trams, buses and trolleybuses). A good understanding of markets is essential if contracting authorities are to develop more realistic and effective tender specifications and provide vendors with a better understanding of public sector needs (OECD, 2019[11]).

*Urban planning and social protection*

Housing and social protection are two other areas prioritised by the government. The total expenditure of Bratislava on social affairs and services procured in 2020 was around EUR 20 million. However, there is a need for more and better housing and social services, especially for vulnerable populations. For instance, the lack of available building plots, slow permit processes and the price of real estate have steered building development towards the rural suburbs. In addition to price issues, housing expansion is causing challenges for the city to provide services without expanding the infrastructure capacity, including waste management, schools, services for the elderly, as well as mobility and transport infrastructure. Improving land use, spatial planning and housing services can support Bratislava in advancing its inclusion agenda. For example, the city is becoming a leader in design contest procedures within the Slovak Republic: it launched half of the 16 design contest procedures that have been published in the Slovak Republic since 2020. These contests aimed at designing projects for the reconstruction and improvement of specific public urban areas. Bratislava could increase efficiency and oversee the implementation of urban planning and social protection policies and their application to wider procurement activities by integrating the different policies and using collaborative procurement groups.

### 1.1.3. The institutional and regulatory framework for public procurement in Bratislava

Bratislava's city government is divided into 13 departments, with a special unit addressing cross-cutting areas. The departments are responsible for organising spatial planning, guiding urban development, protecting the environment, enhancing well-being and social inclusion, as well as providing services related to transport, housing, energy, culture, waste and water management, and air quality. The city has created the Implementation Unit, managed by the mayor's advisors, to advance horizontal priorities, including innovation, mobility, parking and social, green and sustainable policies. However, this unit was recently transferred to the information technology (IT) department and the budget and strategies in place are still following a sectoral approach. To close this gap, the city also created the Metropolitan Institute, which is in charge of working with all departments to align sectoral planning tools and to develop the city's overall strategy.

Public procurement activities are performed within the different departments of the city. Even though there is a specific procurement department (PD) within the management department (1 of the 13 departments of the city), it is not seen as a cross-cutting means to implement the strategic plan of the city. Considering that each department is in charge of its own procurement processes, the PD is mostly perceived as an administrative department merely in charge of supervising procurement procedures. Putting in place a more effective cross-cutting organisational structure to advance public procurement in Bratislava could therefore help improve the efficiency and delivery of services to citizens.

To enhance the strategic role of public procurement in the organisational structure of the city, it is key to map the variety of stakeholders involved in procurement activities at the city level. Seven main stakeholders were identified (see Figure 1.3). Each of these stakeholders have a specific role:

- **Officials from the PD**: They are in charge of developing the tendering procedure and preparing the administrative documents. In 2021, there are 12 procurement experts in this department. According to the city of Bratislava, this number will increase given the needs aggregation strategy that the city is aiming to implement. The turnover rate in the PD has been relatively high in the last six years, which saw six consecutive team leaders. Since January 2021, the city PD was reorganised by introducing two units. This change aims at speeding up procurement processes, as two additional managers will contribute to reviewing those processes.

- **Subject matter experts**: They work in the different departments of the city and they are in charge of developing technical specifications and responsible for contract management (requiring areas).

- **Internal controllers**: They have the authority to control all public procurement procedures of the city, including below threshold procedures.

- **Mayor and mayor's office**: They sign contracts and decide on the adoption of new public procurement directives.

- **Members of the *pravidelna porada primatora***, i.e. members of a regular meeting with the mayor, who serve as an advisory body to the mayor: They are in charge of approving projects and procurement activities that were not initially planned.

- **Officials from the legal affairs department**: They are in charge of reviewing the contracts.

- **Officials from the budget sub-department** (within the department of finance): They are in charge of approving the spending and verifying coherence between needs, the estimated value of the contract and the availability of budgets.

In addition, for the provision of various public services, Bratislava has an ownership interest in several companies that provide services and ensure the implementation of certain policies (municipal enterprise), such as transport, city parking, water and sewage, and waste management services. The City Business Strategy guides these companies. Each of them is responsible for its procurement operations under the supervision of the city and developed its own procurement directives. The Municipal Business Administration Department is leading the co-operation with companies and is working to increase the performance and efficiency of municipal companies and their management. The department has established two different approaches. The first relates to monitoring the management of municipal enterprises. In 2020, companies had to provide regular financial reporting to allow the city to monitor how companies managed their finances and procurement, and whether they complied with the financial plan approved by the city in 2019. The results of this monitoring demonstrated a need to improve the management capacity of municipal companies to increase the quality of public service delivery and spending, and to improve transparency. The second approach aims to improve business management and to utilise synergies with other public services. The city aims to streamline the procurement procedures and provide a better overview and control over public expenditure across companies. Moving forward, the PD could map all stakeholders in charge of procuring services and goods and provide guidance on how other departments could co-ordinate their procurement processes with city companies' procurement. As the city plans to establish a holding with all municipal companies in the future, this mapping of stakeholders involved in procurement and the integration of city companies could contribute to the objectives of the new city strategy discussed in the next section.

**Figure 1.3. City officials involved in public procurement activities in Bratislava**

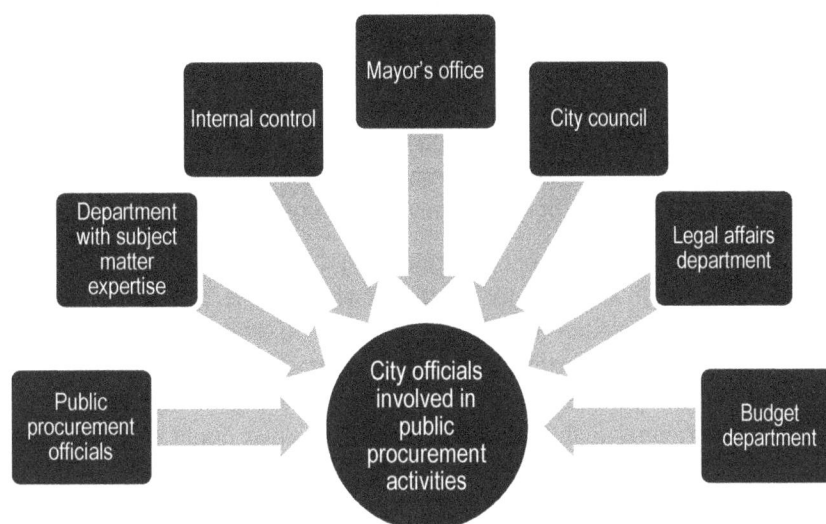

The city of Bratislava's procurement operations are ruled by the national public procurement framework derived from the 2014 European public procurement directives. In addition to the Public Procurement Act (PPA), Bratislava has also developed internal directives on public procurement. The current internal directives were updated in 2018. Bratislava's PD is in the process of developing new directives aiming at improving the procurement process and enhancing the efficiency of the system. The draft directives will reflect systematic procedures covering the whole procurement cycle from needs analysis to the end of the contract (see more details in section 2.1.1). The new directives could play an important role in supporting Bratislava achieving its strategic priorities such as smarter, greener and more inclusive growth.

### 1.1.4. Furthering citizen engagement in budgetary and procurement choices for better services

Public procurement involves the use of public funds that come from taxpayers' money. Therefore, well-governed public procurement can and must play a major role in fostering public sector efficiency and establishing citizens' trust (OECD, 2020[12]). In recent years, civil society participation in the public procurement system has been a critical element in enhancing efficiency, transparency, integrity and accountability in different countries and at different levels of government (OECD, 2020[12]). Compared to the national level, local governments are the closest level of government to citizens, which enables them to implement effective mechanisms to facilitate the participation of citizens and civil society organisations in the procurement system. Those mechanisms can take different forms: i) consultations for reforming the public procurement system; ii) oversight of public procurement spending; and iii) consultations on citizens' needs/procurement plans (OECD, 2020[12]).

To enable consultation on citizens' needs, different mechanisms can be used, such as the organisation of public events and participatory budgeting processes (OECD, 2019[13]). Participatory budgeting processes, for instance, allow for assessing citizens' needs and priorities. They are implemented mainly by subnational governments to empower citizens to vote on local public works projects. Many cities across OECD and non-OECD countries implemented such initiatives, including Lisbon (Portugal), Paris (France), Peñalolén (Chile) and Porto Alegre (Brazil). There are also some examples of participatory budgeting implemented by other cities in the Slovak Republic. For instance, the cities of Poltar and Trnava introduced the concept of participatory budgeting, where citizens are co-creating the investment budget for the city. Up until now, the city of Bratislava did not implement participatory budgeting processes. However, some of its city districts with budget autonomy have implemented such processes for a small share of their budget, ranging between EUR 20 000 and EUR 50 000. Bratislava could consider involving citizens in budgetary choices.

In the city of Bratislava, the most common way of collecting information on citizens' needs is the regular exchange with the members of the municipal assembly. The city also organises events regarding the design of the public space, where they ask citizens to provide feedback. According to the PD, any interested party, including citizens, can send specific requests via the webpage of the city or a smartphone application and the relevant department has an obligation to provide a response. Elected representatives can define their ad hoc priorities and implement them by using a small allocated budget. However, this kind of practice is very limited and does not specifically aim at assessing citizens' needs.

Bratislava has made a substantial investment in digital services in the last few years but without much success and impact on citizens. In order to tackle this challenge, the innovation department has been moved to the IT department. Furthermore, the city is implementing an open data portal, which is providing different types of information to citizens, enabling them to oversee municipal public spending. However, as described in section 2.5.1, the portal includes only past data and does not allow for a timely oversight of public spending and procurement activities. The city of Bratislava could make its portal interactive to advance its engagement with citizens by better understanding their needs and involving them in procurement processes. This could be done not only by providing information for monitoring public spending but also through surveys, consultations on project proposals, etc.

## 1.2. Rethinking the role of public procurement in the strategic vision of the city

### 1.2.1. On the path to a new city strategy for Bratislava in the COVID-19 context

*Taking stock of the current strategy*

The strategy currently in place in Bratislava was developed for the 2010-20 period under the mandate of the former mayor. The strategy focused on five specific policy goals: i) the role of Bratislava as the centre of the metropolitan region; ii) becoming a knowledge-based economy; iii) quality of life and human resources; iv) quality of the environment and urban spaces; and v) mobility and technical infrastructure. As is the case in many cities, the strategy developed by Bratislava did not include any specific mention of the role of public procurement in achieving the city's objectives.

Although there was no measurement framework or any set of indicators to monitor and evaluate the implementation of the strategy, the city was able to track preliminary progress based on four criteria (whether the goal was completely achieved, partially achieved, not achieved or there is no data/no competencies). Monitoring the implementation of the city strategy will be key to ensure that it achieves the desired objectives, and identify challenges and adequate mitigation measures. Bratislava could develop specific, measurable, comparable and timely key performance indicators (KPIs) to evaluate the implementation of its forthcoming strategy. Some of the indicators could be related to the procurement operations of the city (see section 2.3). In the city of Portland, United States (US), for example, the Sustainable Procurement Programme tracks KPIs at the department level to facilitate feedback to bureaux on sustainable procurement performance (City of Portland, 2018[14]). In addition, Bratislava could develop a dashboard on the progress made in the implementation of the strategy and could publish it on line to strengthen stakeholders' engagement.

*Taking stock of the COVID-19 outbreak*

Necessary actions to fight the pandemic increased the pressure on local spending and procurement procedures in Bratislava. For instance, the city launched the construction of a quarantine town with the support of professional, medical and social staff that served 4 000 homeless people just after the pandemic outbreak. In addition, procurement and infrastructure delivery will play a decisive and strategic role in wider governmental responses for the post-crisis recovery (OECD, 2020[15]). According to the city of Bratislava, it is estimated that the COVID-19 pandemic caused direct and indirect losses of more than EUR 25 million in the revenues of the city and its organisations during 2020. Despite the critical macro-economic situation linked to the crisis, Bratislava's city council approved the budget for 2021-23 in December 2020, with the main objective to advance the city's projects, especially in the areas of transport, public spaces and the environment. The majority of these projects will be spent through public procurement operations.

During the initial outbreak, public entities from different levels of government acknowledged the strategic role played by public procurement. COVID-19 has presented all levels of governments with unprecedented challenges in ensuring not only the health of their citizens but also public service continuity (OECD, 2020[16]). Based on the information provided by the city of Bratislava, in 2020, around EUR 1 million was allocated to the procurement of goods, services and infrastructures dedicated to the COVID-19 pandemic (e.g. procurement of masks, gloves, antigen tests and the construction of the quarantine town). Bratislava aims to use its recovery efforts and its new strategy to address long-term challenges, including housing shortages, imbalances in the labour market and environmental pressures. In this respect, Bratislava could spell out the strategic role that public procurement could play in achieving an inclusive, sustainable and smart recovery in its new strategy.

*From taking stock to looking forward: The new city strategy*

The preliminary evaluation of the current strategy has been used to establish a set of short-, medium- and long-term priorities to develop the new city strategy. The city did not develop a specific COVID-19 recovery strategy. However, due to the COVID-19 pandemic, the city of Bratislava had to postpone the launch of the new strategy and redefined short-term priorities to reallocate the budget to emergency responses and recovery and stimulus measures (Table 1.2). The new city strategy (2030) aims to enhance planning and guide future investment needs to improve the quality of life of its citizens. The Metropolitan Institute is in charge of preparing the new city strategy and a related ten-year plan for investments to respond to the urban planning gaps, such as urban deprivation, inequalities in housing, transport, education, health and employment. The city could consider the role of public procurement to implement both the new strategy and the long-term plan. This would be in line with the OECD Principles on Urban Policy (OECD, 2019[17]), welcomed by ministers of OECD countries in March 2019, which underline that public procurement can help cities prepare themselves better for the future.

The long-term plan will identify priorities related to economic development, the administrative structure, the environment, mobility, technical infrastructure, sport, culture and urban development for co-ordinated multi-sectoral planning. Although the city's departments are involved in the process to provide an integrated perspective and prioritise investments, Bratislava does not have a long-lasting history of participatory planning tools to involve districts and citizens. The Metropolitan Institute could use its new strategy to promote an integrated and whole-of-government approach by engaging not only the city departments but also the districts and citizens in the planning process. For example, the metropolitan city of Busan (Korea) has encouraged citizen participation in land use planning and urban regeneration projects (OECD, 2019[18]).

**Table 1.2. Short-, medium- and long-term priorities in the city of Bratislava**

| Short-term priorities | • Containing the COVID-19 crisis<br>• Establishing parking policy (December 2021) |
|---|---|
| Medium-term priorities | • Digital transformation<br>• Localising the United Nations (UN) Sustainable Development Goals (SDGs), including fostering data policy consistency<br>• Advancing the environmental agenda<br>• Tackling social inequalities and improving inclusiveness |
| Long-term priorities | • Establishing an effective strategic decision-making process at the FUA level of the city of Bratislava<br>• Stimulating the local economy<br>• Promoting the circular economy<br>• Implementing the quadruple helix interactive innovation model to strengthen the co-operation with the academy, citizens and their organisations, and boost the local economy and innovation |

Source: Data provided by the Metropolitan Institute, city of Bratislava.

### 1.2.2. Strengthening prioritisation and planning for efficient procurement operations

Strategic planning is one of the main challenges in the city of Bratislava as policy makers are facing trade-offs between short- and medium-term issues. In particular, the city faces challenges regarding co-ordination across departments and with other stakeholders. With the COVID-19 outbreak, the need to strengthen planning and co-ordination among different departments became even more urgent. The pandemic did not only affect the budget of the city but it also jeopardised some of the planned projects and priorities. For the 2021 budget, the city had to review the selection of projects based on the new priorities related to COVID-19. The budgeting process started in the middle of the year 2020 when the finance department collected the needs of the different departments. The finance department requested detailed information from the different departments to prepare the budget (e.g. description of the project, timeline, tentative budget, etc.), translating the needs into operational costs and investments. Strategic planning translates into procurement plans, which provide city officials involved in procurement activities with a 3-years roadmap and help the market understand the needs of the city. However, only 40% of the approved procurement plans on average are executed. The city could therefore take actions to improve the execution of procurement plans. Such actions will also require vertical and horizontal co-ordination to implement the city strategy.

While needs usually exceed the available resources, entities have to set clear criteria to prioritise the different projects. Since the 2008 reform of fiscal decentralisation in the Slovak Republic, Bratislava strongly depends on EU funding. For the programming period 2013-20, the EU finances half of the city's investment in infrastructure, while 45% comes from the state budget and 5% from the city budget. For the new programming period (2021-27), 40% of Bratislava's infrastructure investment will rely on EU funding. The majority of the municipal budget is spent on mandatory expenditures and the priorities mentioned in the city strategy such as transport. However, the rest is spent based on political decisions. For instance, each member of the city council can identify an important project on a small scale and receive the corresponding budget to implement it without following any particular city project or programme. In this context, in 2021, the city established an investment committee that uses specific indicators to prioritise projects. This kind of committee exists in many cities such as London (United Kingdom) and Sacramento, US, as described in Box 1.1. The establishment of such an investment committee in Bratislava could help reinforce accountability and trust in the city government.

## Box 1.1. The role of the investment committee in the city of Sacramento, US

In 2019, the city of Sacramento, California, in the US created an Inclusive Economic and Community Development Investment Committee (IECDIC). The role of the IECDIC is to ensure that city investments are directed towards economic development, job growth and create opportunities for all of the city's residents, including the most vulnerable.

The IECDIC provides the City Manager's Office with advice on the development and review of projects, programmes and policies.

The committee meets regularly, on the first Monday of every month. The meetings are open to the public and the agenda is systematically published on the city of Sacramento's website. During these meetings, the IECDIC discusses various topics such as:

1. The Inclusive Economic Development Strategy and Action Plan.
2. Innovation programmes and projects (e.g. digital inclusion in Sacramento, preparing the ground for start-ups)

The IECDIC can also make non-binding recommendations to the City Manager.

Its work contributes to the prioritisation of city projects and empowers citizens through the organisation of monthly meetings open to the public.

Source: City of Sacramento (2019[19]), *Inclusive Economic and Community Development Investment Committee (IECDIC)*, https://www.cityofsacramento.org/Economic-Development/Inclusive-Economic-Development/Investment-Committee.

## References

City of Portland (2018), *Sustainable Procurement Policy*, City of Portland, United States, https://www.portlandoregon.gov/shared/cfm/image.cfm?id=204110. [14]

City of Sacramento (2019), *Inclusive Economic and Community Development Investment Committee (IECDIC)*, City of Sacramento, United States, https://www.cityofsacramento.org/Economic-Development/Inclusive-Economic-Development/Investment-Committee. [19]

Eurostat (2021), *Population on 1 January by Age Groups and Sex - Functional Urban Areas*, http://appsso.eurostat.ec.europa.eu/nui/show.do?dataset=urb_lpop1&lang=en. [5]

Eurostat (2021), *Regional and Cities Statistics*, Statistical Office of the European Communities, https://ec.europa.eu/eurostat/cache/RCI/#?vis=city.statistics&lang=en. [2]

OECD (2020), "Functional urban areas: Slovak Republic", OECD, Paris, https://www.oecd.org/cfe/regionaldevelopment/Slovak-Republic.pdf. [3]

OECD (2020), "Public procurement and infrastructure governance: Initial policy responses to the coronavirus (Covid-19) crisis", *OECD Policy Responses to Coronavirus (COVID-19)*, OECD, Paris, http://www.oecd.org/coronavirus/policy-responses/public-procurement-and-infrastructure-governance-initial-policy-responses-to-the-coronavirus-covid-19-crisis-c0ab0a96/ (accessed on 11 August 2020). [15]

OECD (2020), "Stocktaking report on immediate public procurement and infrastructure responses to COVID-19", *OECD Policy Responses to Coronavirus (COVID-19)*, OECD, Paris, http://www.oecd.org/coronavirus/policy-responses/stocktaking-report-on-immediate-public-procurement-and-infrastructure-responses-to-covid-19-248d0646/ (accessed on 9 March 2021). [16]

OECD (2020), *Towards a New Vision for Costa Rica's Public Procurement System: Assessment of Key Challenges for the Establishment of an Action Plan*, OECD Publishing, Paris. [12]

OECD (2020), *Transport Bridging Divides*, OECD Urban Studies, OECD Publishing, Paris, https://dx.doi.org/10.1787/55ae1fd8-en. [10]

OECD (2019), *Budgeting and Public Expenditures in OECD Countries 2019*, OECD Publishing, Paris, https://doi.org/10.1787/9789264307957-en (accessed on 18 November 2020). [13]

OECD (2019), "Citizen participation in land-use planning and urban regeneration in Korea", in *The Governance of Land Use in Korea: Urban Regeneration*, OECD Publishing, Paris, https://dx.doi.org/10.1787/77725217-en. [18]

OECD (2019), "OECD Principles on Urban Policy", https://www.oecd.org/cfe/Brochure-OECD-Principles-Urban-Policy.pdf. [17]

OECD (2019), *Reforming Public Procurement: Progress in Implementing the 2015 OECD Recommendation*, OECD Public Governance Reviews, OECD Publishing, Paris, https://dx.doi.org/10.1787/1de41738-en. [11]

OECD (forthcoming), "Unlocking the potential of public procurement in cities", OECD, Paris. [4]

OECD.Stat (2021), *Metropolitan Areas (database)*, OECD, Paris, https://stats.oecd.org/Index.aspx?Datasetcode=CITIES. [6]

OECD/UCLG (2019), *2019 Report of the World Observatory on Subnational Government Finance and Investment – Country Profiles*, https://www.sng-wofi.org/publications/SNGWOFI_2019_report_country_profiles.pdf. [9]

OECD/UCLG (2016), *Country Profile: Slovak Republic*, Subnational Governments Around the World: Structure and Finance, https://www.oecd.org/regional/regional-policy/profile-Slovak-Republic.pdf. [7]

Statistical Office of Slovak Republic (2021), *Municipalities of the Slovak Republic*, http://www.sodbtn.sk/obce/index_kraje.php. [8]

Statistical Office of the Slovak Republic (2021), "DATAcube", https://slovak.statistics.sk/wps/portal/ext/themes/demography/population/indicators/!ut/p/z1/tVFNc5swEP0tOXAUWhCfueFMx3Ybd-p0EhtdOhIIUA0SQYqp--sj0l4607STQ3TanX3a9_Y9TPERU8XOsmVWasV615c0-bZPt9lqFRSQrR5C2Kaf74JP-_16m4f4AVNMK2VH2-FSc8M6ZE4eGOs2VKjSygpIPbBiuH. [1]

# 2. Using public procurement strategically in the city of Bratislava

This chapter provides analysis and recommendations on the strategic use of public procurement in Bratislava. It looks at key elements of the city's public procurement system: processes and measures to enhance the efficiency of procurement outcomes, the use of public procurement to achieve policy objectives such as sustainability and small- and medium-sized enterprise (SME) development, the relevance of measurement frameworks and the capabilities of the procurement workforce. It also looks at transparency and risk management in the procurement process to enhance citizens' trust.

## 2.1. Towards greater efficiency of public procurement activities

An effective response to the needs of citizens in terms of infrastructure and services is one of the main objectives of any public procurement strategy. In Bratislava, public procurement accounted for EUR 145 million in 2019 (39% of the city's expenditures), including around 65 million on infrastructure. Given the volumes at stake, the city administration must ensure good management of public funds to provide citizens with the best possible solutions. The economic shock related to the COVID-19 crisis generated substantial stress on subnational finance in the short, medium and long terms. Furthermore, in the Slovak Republic as in many OECD countries, subnational revenue is already and will continue to be strongly impacted due to reduced tax, tariff/fee- or asset-derived income that is sensitive to economic fluctuations and policy decisions (OECD, 2020[1]).

The OECD *Recommendation of the Council on Public Procurement* stresses the importance of developing processes to drive efficiency throughout the procurement cycle in satisfying the needs of the government and its citizens (OECD, 2015[2]). While public procurement has been considered for many years as an administrative task, in recent years, different levels of governments recognised its strategic role in the delivery of public services and the achievement of different policy objectives related to the environment, innovation and social considerations.

As described in Figure 2.1, in the "traditional" approach to public procurement, efforts are focused on the tendering phase, while the "strategic" approach puts more emphasis on the pre-tendering phase (needs assessment, market research and the development of technical specifications) and the performance of the contract. The following sections aim at assessing the efficiency of procurement processes in Bratislava and providing the city with key recommendations.

## Figure 2.1. Two main approaches to procurement

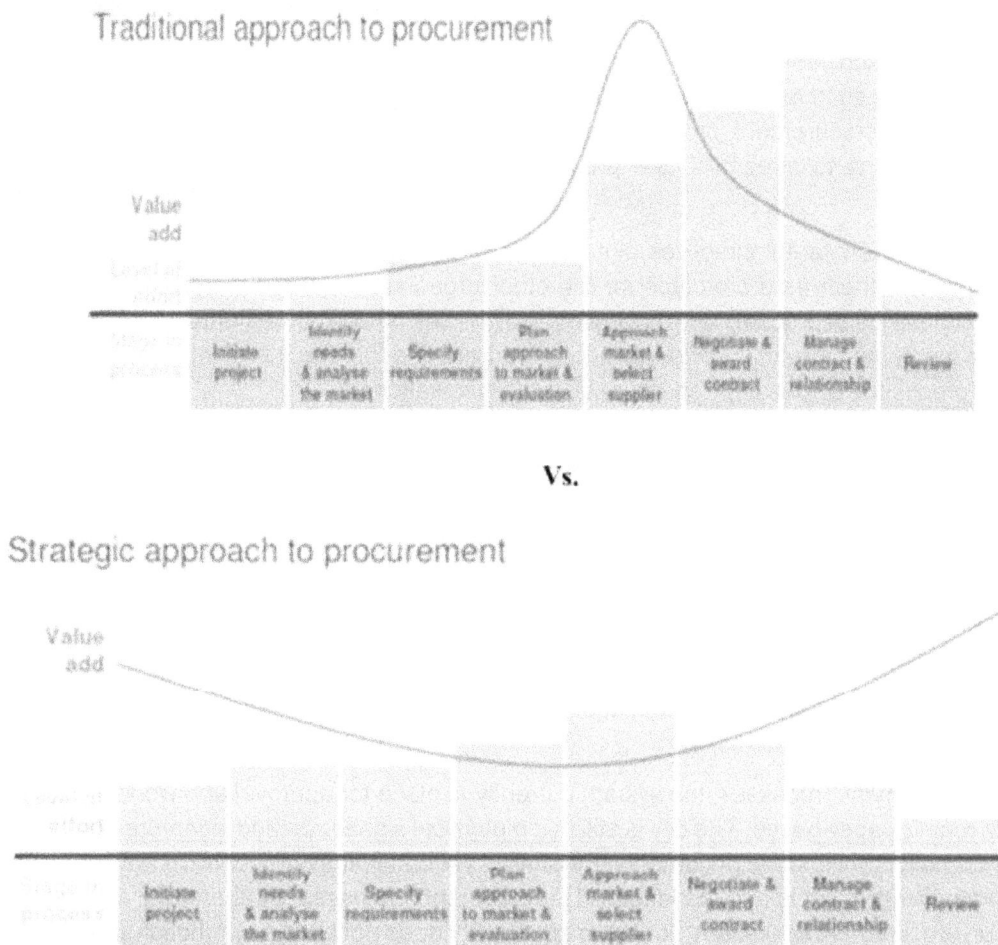

Traditional approach to procurement

Vs.

Strategic approach to procurement

Source: OECD (2017[3]), *Public Procurement in Chile: Policy Options for Efficient and Inclusive Framework Agreements*, https://dx.doi.org/10.1787/9789264275188-en.

### 2.1.1. Streamlining procurement processes

*Reviewing internal procurement processes*

To drive efficiency throughout the procurement cycle, the OECD recommendation calls adherents to streamline the public procurement system. They should "evaluate existing processes and institutions to identify functional overlap, inefficient silos and other causes of waste. Where possible, a more service-oriented public procurement system should then be built around efficient and effective procurement processes and workflows to reduce administrative red tape and costs" (OECD, 2015[2]).

Procurement procedures in contracting authorities derive essentially from the public procurement regulatory framework and their internal directives, as is the case of Bratislava (see section 1.1.3). The procurement process currently in place includes several duplications and inconsistencies that affect its efficiency. For instance, all bidders must sign the conflict of interest form before awarding the contract to a company.

The city of Bratislava is currently in the process of updating its internal procurement directives. In the current process, different stakeholders have a clear role to play, in particular the requiring area, the procurement department (PD), the legal department and the budget department. The main objective is to reduce duplications and identify practical steps that stakeholders involved in the procurement process should follow.

The COVID-19 crisis showed that it was possible to streamline the procurement process. Given the urgent needs for some items such as masks and information technology (IT) equipment in the early stage of the virus outbreak, the procurement process was accelerated and non-essential steps were removed. Continuing such efforts to streamline the procurement processes in the internal directives would be beneficial.

Furthermore, while the internal directives aim to be applied to departments within the city, Bratislava is also planning to use them as a prototype for the other organisations that belong to the city. This would enhance the coherence of procurement processes and policies of all procurements under the responsibility of the city. At the same time, this standardisation could provide the starting point for further streamlining procurement processes across city departments and organisations.

### Further digitalising procurement processes

The OECD recommends the use of digital technologies to improve the public procurement system (OECD, 2015[2]). Digitalising procurement processes implies standardisation, streamlining and integration of processes. This helps reduce administrative costs and processing times. Furthermore, it improves competition and thus value for money (EBRD, 2015[4]).

When analysing the digitalisation of procurement processes, there are two areas to consider: i) the digitalisation of internal processes; and ii) the digitalisation of procurement procedures using external platforms (e-procurement platforms).

On internal procurement processes, the system currently in place for approval and workflows in the city of Bratislava is mainly paper-based. The city is still using physical signatures and signature books to circulate documents formally. While some documents are shared via email, they do not have any legal value. This increases administrative costs and the length of procurement processes. Furthermore, it also affects data availability on procurement operations; for instance, the city does not have any functional central database for contracts and other documents such as market analysis. The PD uses Microsoft Excel files to collect specific procurement data.

However, with the COVID-19 pandemic and social distancing measures, many processes were digitalised, for instance by using digital signatures. The PD and IT departments have discussed this topic in the framework of the update of internal procurement directives. The city should therefore consider digitalising all procurement processes throughout the procurement cycle to enhance the efficiency of the procurement system. In this framework, the city could develop an action plan with a clear timeline for digitalising each phase of the procurement process.

In addition, each city organisation uses a different internal IT system to manage its procurement. It could be beneficial to consider reinforcing interoperability between the different procurement IT systems used by the city organisations and ensure homogeneous processes between them. This decision should be made following a cost-benefit analysis.

Additionally, it is widely documented that e-procurement platforms are changing the way the public and private sectors interact in OECD countries. On top of increased accountability and transparency, it has been estimated that e-procurement can reduce transaction costs by up to 12% and reduce prices paid by governments through its effects on market competition, leading to savings ranging between 5% and 25% (OECD, 2018[5]). In the Slovak Republic, there are 11 e-procurement platform providers. The city of Bratislava has been using two different e-procurement platforms, EVO and Josefine respectively. Recently, an amendment was proposed to make the use of the state platform EVO mandatory (Proebiz, 2021[6]).

### 2.1.2. The key impact of market analysis and needs analysis on the efficiency of the system

The efficiency of public procurement activities requires matching demand with supply. Market analysis and needs analysis are the first step of the procurement process and have a significant impact on the performance of the contract as they affect tender design (Figure 2.2).

**Figure 2.2. The key impact of demand and market analysis on procurement outcomes**

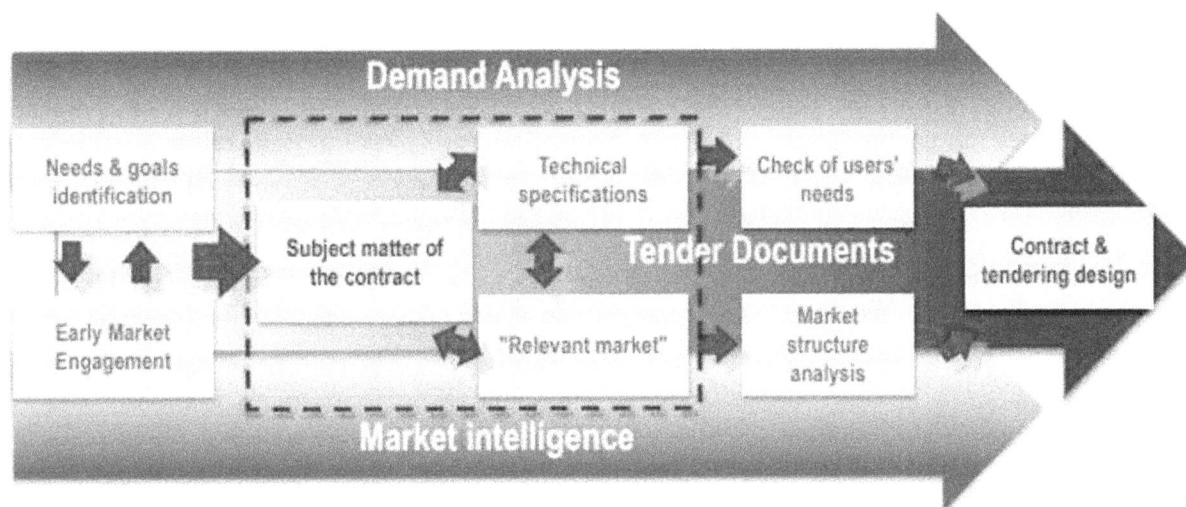

Source: OECD (2018[7]), *Second Public Procurement Review of the Mexican Institute of Social Security (IMSS): Reshaping Strategies for Better Healthcare*, https://dx.doi.org/10.1787/9789264190191-en.

*Enhancing the methodology to undertake needs analysis*

Needs analysis requires identifying the needs of end-users in terms of performance, functionalities, quality and quantity of the solution required. To improve public service delivery, needs analysis should follow a functional and performance-based approach. It should be oriented towards solutions and functions rather than products, services and brands available in the market. To understand the extent to which the market can meet the identified needs, this process should go hand in hand with a sound market analysis (OECD, 2018[7]).

In terms of needs analysis, there are two categories of end users to consider: the public administration for its own operations and citizens as beneficiaries of the public services provided by the entity. As mentioned in section 1.1.4, the city could further improve the collection of information on citizens' needs. In practice, the different requiring areas within the city are the ones that perform the needs analysis. However, Bratislava is not currently following a functional approach.

In Bratislava, needs assessment translates into the development of a procurement plan, which is published in the first term of each year after being approved by the mayor. However, as discussed earlier, only 40% on average of the approved procurement plans have been executed in the last years. The COVID-19 pandemic may explain this low rate of execution of the procurement plan in 2020. However, for the previous years, this low rate could be related to the lack of capacity of requiring areas to undertake this assessment properly. The internal control department of the city identified the lack of adequate planning as one of the key challenges in relation to the procurement process of the city. The city of Bratislava should further investigate the issues related to the low rate of execution of procurement plans and enhance the capacity of requiring areas to undertake this assessment properly, using a functional approach.

*Providing guidance on market analysis*

As described in Figure 2.2, market analysis has a significant impact on the development of technical specifications and the performance of contracts. It aims at identifying the characteristics, capacity and capability of the supply market and their capacity to respond to priorities and policy objectives of the procuring entity.

According to the city of Bratislava, the market analysis process is under the responsibility of requiring areas and is not standardised. However, in practice, those areas can request the support of the PD to undertake it. For instance, the PD analyses the market structure (identification of potential bidders and their characteristics), whereas the requiring areas identify the products, services and public works that respond to their needs. Yet, those two tasks should be done simultaneously and in co-ordination with each other.

Furthermore, the city of Bratislava and its organisations have not yet developed a market analysis template. Such templates enable contracting authorities to streamline their procurement operations and inform their procurement decisions. Usually, information included in the market analysis is related to the market players and the solutions available in the market (Box 2.1). The lack of capacity to undertake market analysis does not only affect the estimated value of tenders (as highlighted by the internal control department) but also the performance of the contracts. Given the benefits of such tools, the city of Bratislava should consider developing a market analysis template and integrate it into its internal public procurement directive.

---

### Box 2.1. Example of information to include in the market analysis template

**Information on market players**

- Structure of the supply chain and typology of the market operators (producers/resellers/system integrators/global service providers, etc.).
- Market shares and dominant positions (monopoly/oligopoly/competitive market).
- Firms (SMEs/large companies; local/national/multinational companies): turnover, business strategy, contract conditions, patents, etc.
- Size of the contract relative to the whole market size.

**Information on solutions available in the market**

- The availability of any alternative products/solutions on the market, which are able to meet the buyer's needs.
- The features, characteristics and market prices of the adequate solutions in the market.
- The market trend (increasing/decreasing prices, technological evolution, etc.).
- The factors influencing market prices (i.e. exchange rate, raw materials price, seasonality, etc.).
- The capacity of the solutions to respond to policy objectives (environmental and social policies, innovation, etc.).

Source: Adapted from OECD (2020[8]), "Training on market analysis", OECD, Paris.

---

To engage the market and collect information, public buyers can use different tools and methods (Box 2.2). Different methods are used depending on the estimated value of the contract but no dedicated and clear guidance has been developed to support requiring areas in choosing the appropriate method. For instance, since 2018, Bratislava has been using preliminary market consultation for some tenders but no criteria have been set to use this methodology. According to the city, this kind of consultation had a positive impact on the procurement strategy adopted and thus on the procurement outcomes. For example, the preliminary market consultation for the procurement of electricity allowed Bratislava to update its pricing strategy, which has a positive impact on procurement outcomes. In 2021, Bratislava planned to organise a "meet the buyer" event to engage further with the private sector. This good practice aims at presenting the upcoming procurement opportunities, providing more information on the objectives to achieve (i.e. green or social aspects), enhancing transparency and giving the market more time to prepare for upcoming procurement opportunities. Therefore, the city of Bratislava should consider providing guidance on the methods to use to engage the market and collect information in its public procurement directive. In order to demonstrate the added value of such practices, the city of Bratislava could collect evidence on improvements related to procurement outcomes, namely in terms of quality and savings. The monitoring process could be standardised to allow further evaluation of performance in diverse procurement topics.

---

### Box 2.2. How to engage the market and collect information on the market?

Different methodologies can be used to engage the market.

**Direct engagement mechanisms**

- Publish procurement plan.
- Organise public events to meet with suppliers.
- Meet with key suppliers (taking into account integrity risks).
- Request for quotation (RfQ)/questionnaires.

**Getting information from third parties**

- Commission a consultant (public and transparent selection).
- Use market analysis or sector study reports published by specialised companies or trade unions.
- Consult other contracting authorities with experience in similar procurement.

Source: OECD (2020[8]), "Training on market analysis", OECD, Paris.

---

### 2.1.3. Reaping the benefits of the aggregation of needs to enhance the efficiency of Bratislava's procurement activities

*Towards further needs aggregation with other contracting authorities*

Aggregating needs is a key lever to enhance the efficiency of public procurement systems. This holds particularly true in times of fiscal austerity when all levels of governments are focusing efforts on rationalising public spending (OECD, 2019[9]). The main benefits of needs aggregation are: i) the achievement of economies of scale through a higher procurement volume which translates into lower prices and/or better quality; and ii) the achievement of administrative savings by reducing duplications. There are different ways of aggregating needs: through centralisation of procurements from different contracting authorities usually with the lead of a single contracting authority or by doing joint procurements between two or more contracting authorities. Those tools are identified as key efficiency tools in the OECD *Recommendation of the Council on Public Procurement* (2015[2]). The aggregation of needs requires taking into account key factors such as the existence of homogeneous needs and the impact on market conditions, namely on competition, vendor locking and SMEs.

The Slovak public procurement law enables contracting authorities to aggregate their needs through centralisation (Section 15 of the Public Procurement Act [PPA]) or joint procurement arrangements (Section 16 of the PPA).

The city of Bratislava owns 44 organisations such as the waste management company and the transport company. The public procurement system in the city is mostly decentralised. The organisations belonging to the city conduct their own procurement as they are independent contracting authorities. Due to their lack of capacity on public procurement, these organisations tend to rely extensively on external consultants to support them in conducting procurement procedures, which in turn makes the cost of procurement higher. In a 2019 survey conducted by the city of Bratislava on areas in which city organisations would consider external support, public procurement was ranked first.

In some cases, the needs of the city of Bratislava and the ones of the city organisations are aggregated and presented to the market via joint procurement arrangements. Among the procurement categories subject to the aggregation of needs are energy (such as electricity and gas), meal vouchers and office supplies. However, no data are available on the share of procurement spending they represent. City organisations have generally positive feedback on their experience and there is potential to undertake joint procurement in other categories, in particular IT goods and services. Given the benefits of needs aggregation, the city is considering furthering the use of joint procurement arrangements within city organisations in other procurement categories such as in the digital fields. However, no specific methodology has been developed to inform decisions on the potential aggregation of needs of relevant procurement categories. Furthermore, managers of the major procurement departments across city organisations used to meet on a regular basis and the procurement procedures of these organisations are approved by the city that also receives their procurement plans. Therefore, the city should consider undertaking an analysis of procurement spending and the procurement plans of each organisation. This could help identify potential procurement categories where needs aggregation could contribute to enhancing the efficiency of procurement outcomes. Regular meetings with the procurement managers of the different city organisations can also be the occasion to discuss the potential of aggregating the needs of some procurement categories.

In addition to city organisations, joint procurement arrangements can be established with other contracting authorities, including those from different levels of government. The city of Bratislava has not implemented such arrangements so far but it could explore the possibility of joining forces with surrounding municipalities (inter-municipal co-ordination), the region of Bratislava and city districts that are independent of the city to improve the efficiency of procurement operations. For instance, inter-municipal co-operation arrangements can enable the internalisation of externalities in the management of services and reap economies of scale in different areas, including utility services (water, waste, energy, etc.), transport infrastructure and telecommunication. This is particularly beneficial for municipalities within the same functional urban area (FUA) (see section 1.1.1) (OECD, forthcoming[10]). According to the city of Bratislava, legislative changes supporting inter-municipal co-operation within FUAs are needed because municipalities are currently competing against each other to obtain financial resources rather than co-operating. For example, in the Slovak Republic, at the local level, a high share of public investments are financed by European Union (EU) funds and the allocation of funds is based on the assessment of each demand. The city is currently preparing an integrated territorial strategy in co-operation with the region of Bratislava. The city could use the preparation of this strategy to explore possibilities for joining forces with the region on procurement activities to enhance the efficiency of public spending.

*Enhancing the use of collaborative procurement instruments*

Collaborative procurement instruments are among the most commonly used tools to drive efficiency and cost-effectiveness. They open the door to streamlined procurement processes, reduce duplication of administrative costs and increase government purchasing power. These instruments include framework agreements and dynamic purchasing systems (DPS) (OECD, 2017[3]), which are mentioned in the Slovak PPA.

A framework agreement means an agreement between a fixed number of one or more contracting authorities and one or more economic operators, with the purpose of establishing the terms governing contracts to be awarded during a given period, in particular with regard to price and, where appropriate, the quantity envisaged (EU, 2014[11]). Once awarded, no additional economic operators can join a framework agreement . A DPS is somehow a framework agreement which potential suppliers can join any time during its period of validity, thus enabling further competition over time. The DPS can streamline procurement for both suppliers and authorities. The contract award process can also be conducted more rapidly than under other procedures. A DPS offers flexibility in fast-paced, constantly changing markets (OECD, 2019[12]). The use of needs aggregation coupled with those collaborative instruments enables to achieve further efficiency gains.

Aware of the benefits of those instruments, the city of Bratislava has implemented eight framework agreements (i.e. electricity, gas, meal vouchers, office supplies, etc.) and four DPS on furniture, IT hardware and public works for the street lighting system. However, no data is available on the procurement volume they represent. The city also implemented a DPS for COVID-19 related products. While no data are available on the procurement volume they represent, this strategy was beneficial given the unexpected nature of the crisis and the regular new entrants in the market for COVID-19 products such as masks. Beyond the city of Bratislava, its organisations are also starting to use DPS and framework agreements and the recent framework agreements and DPS launched by Bratislava mention the city organisations as potential beneficiaries.

In general, the decision to use those instruments depends mainly on the subject matter of the contract. The 2014 European directives mention that the DPS should be used for commonly used or off-the-shelf products, works or services which are generally available on the market (EU, 2014[11]). According to the city of Bratislava, these categories of goods, services and works are not strictly defined in the Slovak Republic and they are narrowly interpreted by the Public Procurement Office (PPO). This limits the use of DPS in the country. At the national level, the PPO could provide contracting authorities with further guidance on the procurement categories where a DPS can be used.

The city is aiming to further its use of DPS in the upcoming months. Yet, to reap the benefits of those efficiency tools, the first step for contracting authorities is to have a clear understanding of the areas of spending and the frequency of need. Currently, no comprehensive data are available on all of the areas of spending. While construction works and maintenance are considered as top areas of spending, no collaborative procurement instruments are used in these categories, except for public works for street lighting. To enhance the efficiency of its procurement outcomes, the city of Bratislava could consider undertaking a public procurement spending review to assess the amounts spent in each procurement category. This will enable the city to identify procurement categories where collaborative procurement instruments could be used by the different departments and city organisations.

### 2.1.4. Integrating the concept of value for money in procurement processes and improving competition

How cities spend taxpayers' money, how they deliver services and how they make strategic investment decisions makes procurement an increasingly important tool to go beyond the economic aspects of "value for money". In the past years, the concept of value concerning public spending has been evolving to encompass a wider range of considerations such as quality, environmental and social considerations (OECD, forthcoming[10]). To ensure the integration of the concept of value for money in procurement processes, it is key to have a comprehensive understanding of the procurement cycle and choose the right qualification and award criteria. Following a proper planning phase, including needs assessment and market research, those criteria have a direct impact on competition and thus on the performance of contracts.

*Choosing the right qualification and award criteria*

As highlighted in the Slovak PPA, qualification criteria should be "transparent, objective and non-discriminatory". In the city of Bratislava, the procurement department (PD) collaborates with subject matter experts to define qualification criteria. To ensure that suppliers do not fall in one of the exclusion grounds foreseen in the PPA, the PD checks the "list of economic operators", which contains information at the national level about those operators, to prove that there are no grounds for exclusion. In addition, contracting authorities have to check the national register of references of economic operators managed by the PPO. This register includes information on the previous experiences of economic operators contracting with the public sector. However, contracting authorities do not always fill it in appropriately. If a supplier does not get a score of 100%, the contracting authority needs to prove why and the process is burdensome – it appears that very few entities comply with this proofing exercise and prefer to put a score of 100%. To overcome this issue, the PPO should provide a clear methodology with adequate criteria for filling the past experience of suppliers. Criteria could include the level of compliance of the items purchased with the technical specifications, compliance with the initial delivery timeline, etc. Furthermore, the PPO should provide guidelines on how to use this information, including the "acceptable threshold" to contract with a supplier.

In terms of award criteria, Section 44 of the Slovak PPA offers three options: i) the best price-quality ratio (BPQR); ii) life cycle costing (LCC); and iii) the lowest price. The use of BPQR criteria enables contracting authorities to assess bids not only based on the price criterion but also on other aspects such as quality, technical merit, social and environmental characteristics, qualification and experience of supplier staff, after-sales service and technical assistance and delivery conditions. Furthermore, using the BPQR criteria along with the LCC method can also support innovation outcomes and enhance competition (OECD, 2019[13]). Box 2.3 provides more guidance on the use of BPQR criteria.

According to the PPO, the use of BPQR criteria in the Slovak Republic is one of the main challenges of the procurement system. Slovak contracting authorities still mostly rely on the lowest price criteria to award public contracts. Data provided by the PPO show that between 2016 and 2020, only 16% of procurement opportunities included BPQR criteria, representing 13% of the total procurement volume. The PPO, with the support of the OECD, is currently working on a strategy and guidelines to enhance the use of BPQR criteria in the Slovak Republic.

---

**Box 2.3. Using BPQR criteria in public procurement tenders**

BPQR is used where value for money can be assessed as a balance between price and quality. The term "value for money" means the optimum combination between the various criteria (cost-related and non-cost-related criteria) that together meet the contracting authority's requirements.

However, the elements that constitute the optimum combination of these various criteria differ from procurement to procurement and depend on the outcomes required by the contracting authority. Using BPQR, as opposed to the lowest price criterion, presents a series of advantages. It allows contracting authorities to take into account qualitative considerations. The BPQR criteria are typically used when quality is important for the contracting authority. Some cases where it may be considered appropriate to use BPQR are as follows.

- **The procurement of supplies**: For public supply contracts that involve significant and specialised product installation and/or maintenance and/or user training activities, the contract

---

award is usually made on the basis of BPQR criteria. For this type of contract, in fact, quality is generally particularly important.

- **The procurement of works**: For works designed by the tenderer, BPQR criteria are often used.
- **The procurement of services**: For the procurement of consultancy services and more generally intellectual services, quality is normally very important. Experience has shown that when procuring this type of service, the best results in terms of the best value for money are achieved when BPQR criteria are used.

Source: European Commission (EC, 2015[14]), "Public Procurement Guidance for practitionners", http://dx.doi.org/10.2776/578383.

In the city of Bratislava, the most used methodology to assess tenders is also the lowest price. Data provided by the PPO on procedures published between 1 April 2016 and 30 May 2020 show that the use of BPQR criteria decreased in terms of both the value and the number of procedures (Figure 2.3). However, according to the PD, the data provided by PPO are overestimating the use of BPQR criteria. In addition, when contracting authorities were using the "delivery time" criterion in their tenders, they were considered as implementing the BPQR approach; this practice might explain the good performance in terms of the use of BPQR criteria in 2016. The PD mentioned that the low uptake of BPQR criteria is linked to several factors, including the willingness of requiring areas, their capacity and capabilities to adopt this approach, and market preparedness.

Furthermore, using the lowest price criterion can have an impact on the quality of the procured services and products. The city of Bratislava highlighted its willingness to implement further BPQR criteria, as this will be also reflected in the new version of the internal directives that the city is currently updating. For instance, in the draft directives and for procurement activities with an estimated value above EUR 50 000, the city aims at creating a working group comprised of the PD, the environmental department and the social department to review and discuss the relevant criteria to apply. The city of Bratislava is therefore moving in the right direction by including a section on BPQR criteria in the next edition of internal procurement directives. Additionally, Bratislava could consider raising the awareness of the different requiring areas about the importance of using BPQR criteria. For example, it could present the advantages of its use, including concrete examples of its application in the city organisations and bring in good practices from other contracting authorities in other parts of the Slovak Republic.

**Figure 2.3. The use of BPQR/MEAT criteria in the city of Bratislava, 2016-20**

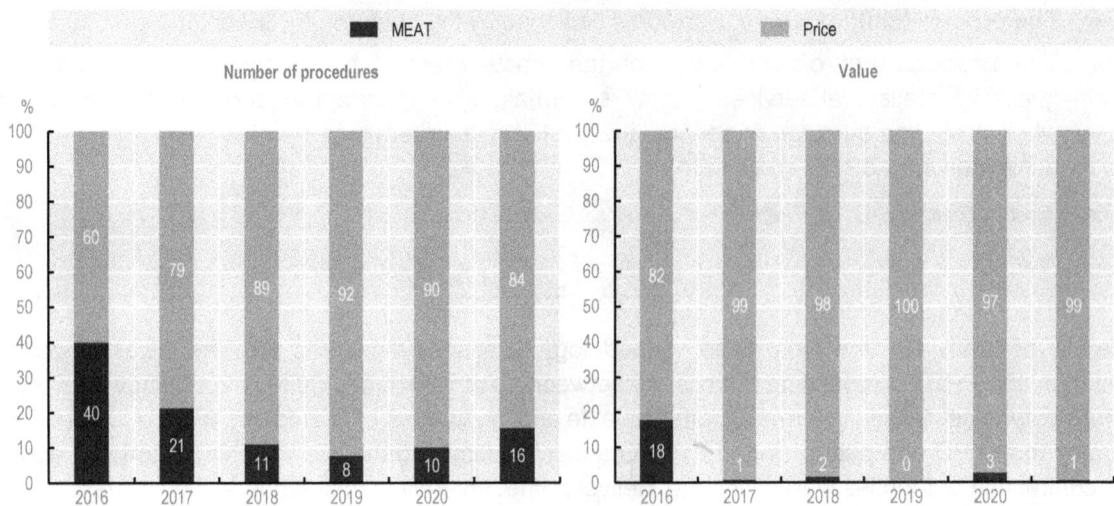

Note: MEAT means most economically advantageous tender. In the figure this means the use of BPQR.
Source: Data provided by the PPO.

Furthermore, when evaluating prices in procurement procedures, it is strongly recommended to use the LCC approach, as this allows for a comprehensive understanding and quantification of the product or service relevance and usage. When procuring a product, service or work, contracting authorities have to pay a "purchase price"; however, this price is just one of the cost elements in the whole process of purchasing, owning and disposing of. LCC means considering all of the costs that will be incurred during the lifetime of the product, work or service (EC, 2020[15]). This includes: i) purchase price and all associated costs (delivery, installation, insurance, etc.); ii) operating costs, including energy, fuel and water use, spares and maintenance; iii) end-of-life costs, such as decommissioning or disposal; and iv) costs imputed to environmental externalities (OECD, 2020[16]). While this approach has never been implemented in Bratislava, it could be combined with the use of BPQR criteria. The city of Bratislava should consider assessing the opportunity of adopting an LCC approach in its procurement operations with significant operating and end-of-life costs. This could entail developing tailored pilot projects to test the LCC methodology and familiarise practitioners and requiring areas with this concept.

### *Better competition for enhanced value for money*

The value that procurement can deliver hinges on the ability to generate competition between businesses. International institutions such as the EU and OECD actively encourage the use of competitive tendering to enhance value for money and innovation, while ensuring that the use of taxpayer funds is free from corruption and other integrity breaches (OECD, 2018[17]). Furthermore, as mentioned earlier (see section 2.1.1), there is also clear evidence on the impact of the use of electronic platforms on the competition.

Competition for a specific contract depends on different parameters, including: i) the procurement method used; ii) the tender documentation (including award and qualification criteria and technical specification); iii) the size of the contract and the adoption of allotment strategies; and iv) the deadline for submitting bids.

In terms of procurement procedures above the threshold, according to the city of Bratislava, the vast majority were launched via a competitive process (open tenders, competitive dialogue and design contests). In 2019 and 2020, there were less than five direct awards and only one restricted tender. The average number of bidders above the EU threshold has increased since 2018, moving from 1.75 bidders in 2018 to 5.44 bidders in 2020. However, the internal control department highlighted contract fragmentation, which reinforces the recommendation on enhancing needs analysis and the planning phase.

All procurement opportunities below the threshold have to be published in the official journal. For low-value contracts (below EUR 70 000 for goods and services, EUR 180 000 for public works, EUR 260 000 for the procurement of special services), the previous Slovak PPA mandated contracting authorities to ask for three quotes from companies in order to award a contract. However, the new PPA does not provide any specific guidance. Despite this change, contracting authorities keep using the three quotes rule in their procurement operations and directives. Since 2018, to enhance further competition, the city of Bratislava went beyond the legal requirements and is targeting five quotes on average. The city should therefore continue its efforts to enhance competition for below threshold contracts.

As mentioned earlier (see section 2.1.2) improving access and enhancing competition is also linked to the time that potential suppliers have to submit their bids. Contracting authorities should carefully choose the number of advertising days (or submission deadline) so that interested suppliers have sufficient time to be informed and prepare their bids. While the PPA sets the minimum number of days for bid submission, the adequate number of days will depend on the complexity of the procurement operation. Therefore, market analysis is pivotal to set an adequate submission deadline, as contracting authorities can understand the specificities of the relevant market and the time it will require to prepare and submit a bid. Based on information from the zIndex platform, an NGO initiative that intends to evaluate the quality of contracting authorities in the Slovak Republic, the analysis of a sample of 28 tenders showed that for 43% of them, the initial submission deadlines were extended (zIndex, 2020[18]). This fact highlights the need to reinforce market analysis and the capacity to define an adequate submission deadline.

## 2.2. Using public procurement to achieve strategic objectives

Public procurement is a crucial pillar of service delivery for governments, affecting citizens' lives in areas ranging from energy efficiency to health services. Because of the sheer volume of spending it represents (12.6% of gross domestic product [GDP] in OECD countries in 2019 (OECD, 2021[19])), well-governed public procurement plays a major role in fostering public sector efficiency and establishing citizens' trust. In addition, governments are increasingly using public procurement as a strategic tool for achieving complementary policy goals such as environmental protection, innovation, job creation and the development of SMEs (OECD, 2019[13]). The strategic role of public procurement to achieve these policy goals translates into the development and implementation of dedicated strategies and policies (Figure 2.4).

The OECD Recommendation on Public Procurement contains guiding principles to assist governments in achieving the right balance between the primary procurement objective and complementary policy objectives so that public procurement systems support the achievement of broader outcomes (OECD, 2015[2]). Regions, cities and rural areas are well placed to enable the strategic use of public procurement through local networks and actions that complement national frameworks. They are also the places where trade-offs between different objectives are felt the strongest since residents can directly experience the local benefits of such policies (OECD, 2020[20]).

Using procurement in a strategic way is a relatively recent concept in the city of Bratislava. However, recognising the importance of its purchasing power, the city is willing to advance the strategic use of public procurement.

**Figure 2.4. Existence of a strategy/policy to pursue complementary policy objectives in public procurement at the national level**

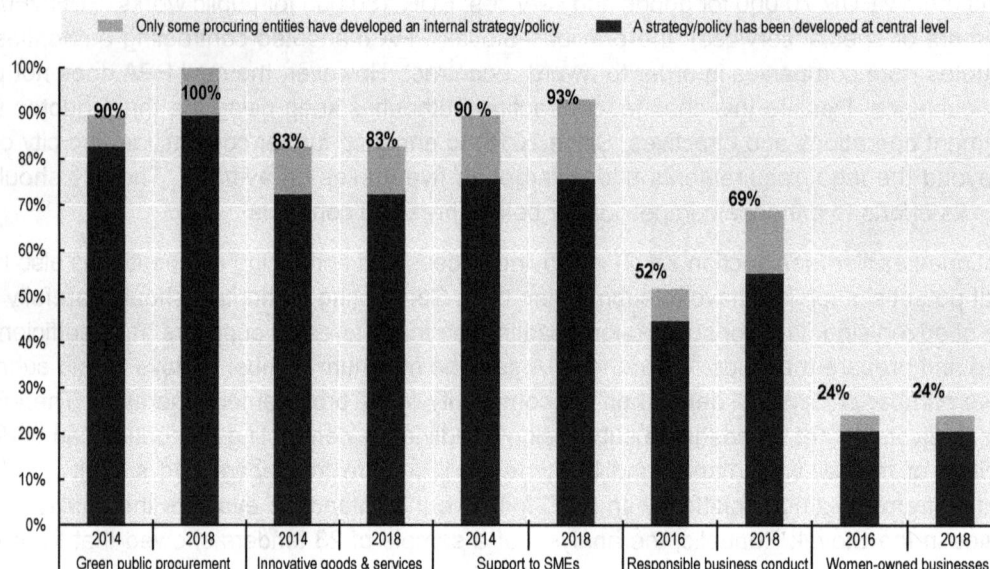

Source: OECD (2019[13]), *Reforming Public Procurement: Progress in Implementing the 2015 OECD Recommendation*, https://doi.org/10.1787/1de41738-en.

## 2.2.1. Integrating sustainability considerations in procurement processes

The COVID-19 crisis reinforced the need to transition towards greener and more inclusive economies to build a better future for citizens. All levels of government, including cities, have a responsibility in this transition and could use the appropriate tools and mechanisms to achieve these goals.

In this context, Bratislava is using the United Nations (UN) Sustainable Development Goals (SDGs) as a framework to prepare its new city strategy (see section 1.2.1). Bratislava is committed to producing its voluntary local review on SDG implementation at the city level. Furthermore, the city is participating in the URBACT project Global Goals for Cities, which aims to elaborate an integrated action plan to implement the SDGs. This URBACT project supports the development of the new city strategy. More specifically, this project aims at integrating the 2030 agenda and its targets in policy planning by designing, implementing, monitoring and reviewing appropriate measures. However, Bratislava is not using procurement as a tool to achieve the SDGs. The city could benefit from introducing, for example, sustainability criteria in future procurement processes.

Bratislava is also committed to climate action since 2008. This commitment translated into the development of a strategy on adaptation to climate change in 2014, with an action plan for 2017-20. The city's environmental agenda will be supported by the integrated territorial investments (ITI) under the new EU programming period (2021-27). Bratislava is focusing on climate adaptation and mitigation measures, as well as the creation of a new protected floodplain forest area around the Danube River. In addition, Bratislava has launched a circular economy strategy in March 2021.

Public procurement can be leveraged to achieve sustainability in line with the strategic vision of the city. Different cities across the globe have recognised the strategic role of public procurement to achieve these goals. For instance, in 2018, Groningen, the Netherlands, identified procurement as one of its priority areas to develop its sustainable and circular vision. City employees are being trained to use green public procurement (GPP) for purchasing in a circular way (OECD, 2020[21]). In Valladolid, Spain, the city has approved Municipal Ordinance 1/2018 to Promote Social Efficient Procurement: Strategic, Exhaustive and Sustainable. The ordinance includes environmental dimensions, entailing that the subject and pricing of municipal contracts should consider life cycle criteria or the most innovative, efficient and sustainable solutions. Expected impacts are related to reducing air pollution, using recycled material and promoting recycling (OECD, 2020[22]).

While the city of Bratislava has not clearly identified public procurement as a strategic lever to achieve sustainability, it could leverage the potential of public procurement and use specific mechanisms described in Figure 2.5 such as award criteria and technical specifications. Those mechanisms are also foreseen in the Slovak PPA.

## Figure 2.5. Mechanisms to embed environmental and social aspects in procurement activities

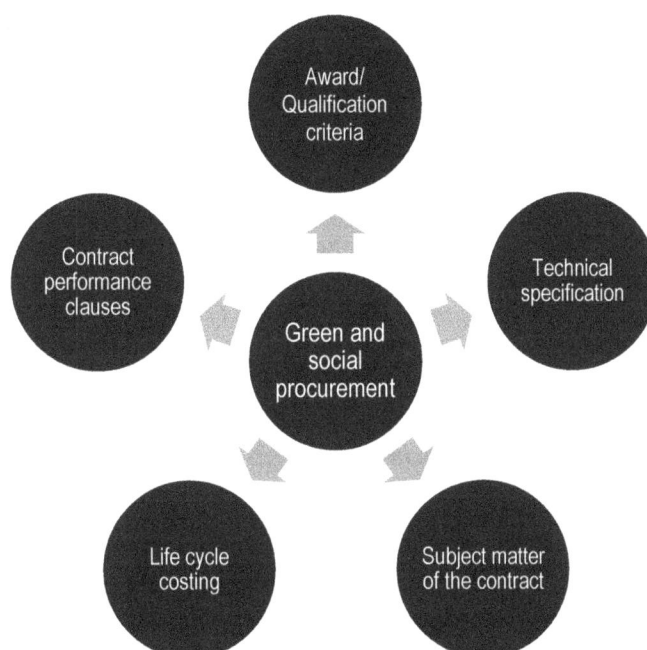

Furthermore, since 2020, a target of 6% of tenders (above and below threshold) with social elements have been introduced in the Slovak Republic for all contracting authorities. However, despite the enabling regulatory framework, the use of such mechanisms in practice to achieve environmental and social objectives remains relatively limited. Aware of those challenges, the PPO prepared a set of guidelines for the implementation of social, green and innovative public procurement in 2017 and a strategy on social procurement in 2021.

The city of Bratislava started implementing some of these mechanisms in 2018. Since then, it aims at integrating more environmental and social considerations in procurement processes when launching new procedures. However, no data are available on the share of procurement integrating green or social aspects. The draft of the upcoming internal directives is already including specific policies on public procurement such as those related to "responsible procurement" (which includes green and social aspects). The city of Bratislava should pursue its efforts to mainstream sustainability in its procurement operations and ensure that all of the mechanisms to embed sustainability in procurement activities are clearly reflected in the internal directives.

Furthermore, the environmental and social departments are collaborating with the PD, especially when it comes to their own procurement and they are committed to enhancing the use of strategic procurement in their procurement opportunities or those under their supervision. For instance, the environmental department sets key performance indicators (KPIs) on GPP for the waste management company. However, there is no direct and institutionalised co-operation between the environmental and social departments with the required areas such as the transport department. As mentioned in section 2.1.4, in the draft of new internal directives, for procurement activities with an estimated value above EUR 50 000, Bratislava aims at creating a working group comprised of the PD, the environmental department and the social department to review and discuss the relevant award criteria. The knowledge of those departments should be further leveraged in the internal directives. Their engagement should not be limited to defining award and qualification criteria but should cover all of the mechanisms aiming at embedding sustainability in procurement operations, such as technical specifications, qualification criteria and the use of LCC.

The capacity of the procurement workforce to support the strategic use of public procurement should also be considered (OECD, 2015[2]). In this context, different cities such as Barcelona committed to providing council staff with dedicated training on sustainable procurement (EC, 2016[23]). Different stakeholders within the city of Bratislava called for further capacity-building activities to advance the environmental and social agenda. In order to do so, the city of Bratislava could consider providing training activities to different stakeholders of the public procurement system on the use of public procurement to achieve the sustainability agenda.

Embedding sustainability in procurement processes requires engaging the market. Different stakeholders in the city of Bratislava perceive the readiness of the market as one of the main challenges in the uptake of more strategic public procurement. In this regard, some initiatives have already been launched, such as the co-operation of the social affairs department with the social entrepreneurship alliance and the planning of a conference on socially responsible procurement. The city of Bratislava could consider organising further activities with the private sector to raise the awareness of economic operators and advance its vision in terms of sustainable procurement.

### 2.2.2. Stimulating the local economy through public procurement

*Using public procurement to support SME development*

As in most of the EU-OECD countries, the Slovak economy relies heavily on SMEs, which represent more than 70% of employment and 55% of value-added in the country. SMEs are active in different sectors where public procurement can play an important role (Figure 2.6). Data provided by the PPO show that on average between 1 April 2016 and 30 May 2020, 69% of procedures were awarded to SMEs, representing not even half of the total procurement volume (40%).

Measures and tools used by governments to enhance SME development include financial measures, allotment strategies and administrative simplification.

On financial measures, the average payment deadline in the city of Bratislava is 30 days, which is in line with EU directives. In addition, in line with internal good practices, the Slovak PPA enables the direct payment of subcontractors and the use of advance payment. The use of advance payments is particularly relevant when the execution of a contract is relatively long. This affects smaller firms in particular as it can impact their liquidity (OECD, 2018[24]). However, in practice, advanced payments are never used in the city of Bratislava. In line with the regulatory framework, the city could analyse the relevance of integrating advance payments in its internal directives for specific types of contracts.

Section 46 of the Slovak PPA also provides the possibility to require a bid bond from bidders. For above threshold tenders, bid bonds should not exceed 5% of the estimated value of the contract and must not be higher than EUR 500 000. For below threshold tenders, the bid bond should be less than 3% of the estimated value of the contract and less than EUR 100 000. As Bratislava is aware of the impact of bid bonds on the level of participation of economic operators, in particular of SMEs, in its procurement operations, it rarely requires bidders to provide a bid bond.

## Figure 2.6. SME density by sector, 2016

Percentage of total business employment in the sector

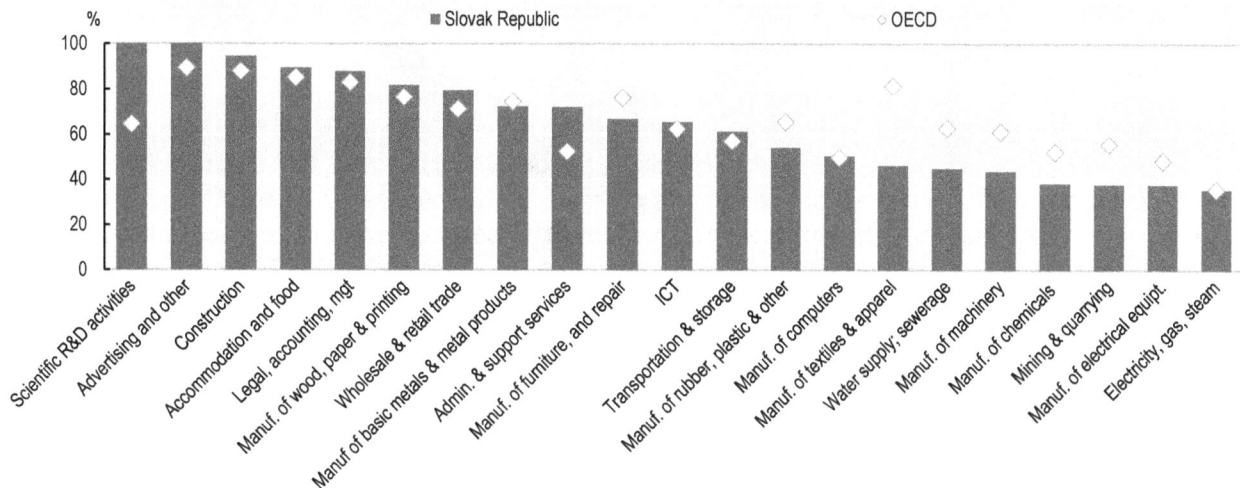

Source: OECD (2019[25]), "Slovak Republic", https://doi.org/10.1787/53572c0d-en (accessed on 6 April 2021).

One of the main measures used to enhance SME access to public procurement opportunities is the implementation of an allotment strategy, which the city of Bratislava is applying. The zIndex platform shows that 17% of a sample of 46 tenders included an allotment strategy in 2020 (zIndex, 2020[18]). Based on these encouraging results, the city could further expand its allotment strategies in its procurement operations. Furthermore, as described in section 2.1.3, the city is using more and more DPS. The use of DPS improves accessibility for SMEs throughout the duration of the contract (NHS, 2021[26]).

Additionally, as mentioned in section 2.5.1, the city of Bratislava goes beyond the regulatory framework on transparency obligations and also publishes low-value contracts. Given the size of low-value contracts, this good practice enhances competition and improves procurement opportunities for SMEs.

*Using public procurement for innovation to respond to citizens' needs*

Innovation in the European public procurement context means "'the implementation of a new or significantly improved product, service or process, including but not limited to production, building or construction processes, a new marketing method, or a new organisational method in business practices, workplace organisation or external relations *inter alia* with the purpose of helping to solve societal challenges or to support the Europe 2020 strategy for smart, sustainable and inclusive growth" (EU, 2014[11]). Public procurement for innovation has the potential to improve productivity and inclusiveness if used strategically as targeted, demand-side innovation policies to meet societal needs. For example, it can anticipate future investments to address existing or future societal challenges; or it may allow potential vendors to enter the market with new, innovative goods or services, thus encouraging innovative solutions to pressing challenges (OECD, 2017[27]). In addition, the COVID-19 crisis has changed the way people live and work and provided an opportunity to upscale innovation and the use of digital tools in cities (OECD, 2020[28]). Using public procurement for innovation could help Bratislava address the impacts of the pandemic, future shocks and global megatrends improve service delivery and spur economic growth.

Bratislava has developed innovation activities and partnerships to promote innovation capacity with other public agencies, private firms, not-for-profit organisations and city residents/resident associations. However, according to the OECD/Bloomberg Philanthropies survey on innovation capacity in cities , Bratislava did not have an explicit innovation strategy (OECD/Bloomberg, 2018[29]). In addition to its new strategy underway, Bratislava is currently in the process of developing an innovation strategy focusing on how to use innovation to promote sustainable development and make Bratislava smarter in the COVID-19 context. The city could consider highlighting in the innovation strategy the strategic role that public procurement could play, considering its impact on economies and societies.

According to the city, the innovativeness of businesses in Bratislava is relatively low. As cities are at the forefront of public service delivery, they are also laboratories for innovative products and solutions aiming at enhancing citizens' well-being (OECD, forthcoming[10]). Moreover, innovation at the local level is closely connected to the smart city agenda of cities since the "smart city" concept initially referred to initiatives that use digital and information and communication technology (ICT)-based innovation to improve the efficiency of urban services and generate new economic opportunities in cities (OECD, 2020[30]; forthcoming[10]). These challenges highlight the pressing need to develop and implement public procurement procedures that spur innovation at the local level.

Public procurement for innovation is an opportunity to solve public sector challenges that span across different levels of governments and sectors. Consequently, public procurement does not only prioritise "governance"-related issues; it aims to help governments understand a complex system comprised of innovation value chains, which have local, national and international ramifications. Taking into account the challenges and obstacles concerning the development and implementation of strategic procurement for innovation, the OECD has identified nine action areas that should be present in any sound procurement for innovation agenda. As described in Table 2.1, many of these actions can be implemented by subnational governments given their role and autonomy. Strategic procurement for innovation combines issues that usually fall under the remit of different governmental bodies both at the local and national levels (e.g. policy making, purchasing, budgeting and scientific research).

**Table 2.1. Nine action areas for a sound procurement for the innovation agenda**

| Action areas | Central government | Subnational/ local government |
|---|:---:|:---:|
| Embed policy strategies with defined targets within any national, subnational and regional innovation policy. | X | X |
| Set up a legal framework, including understandable definitions, guidelines and templates to facilitate its implementation. | X | |
| Designate "transformational" leaders with specialised knowledge to create skilled multidisciplinary teams, so as to encourage sound management. | X | X |
| Dedicate sufficient budgets, funds and other financial incentives, as lack of financial support is one of the main challenges in procurement for innovation. | X | X |
| Promote professionalisation by providing specific training to build staff capabilities and skills, setting up multidisciplinary teams and competency centres focused on public procurement for innovation. | X | X |
| Raise awareness by publishing good practice cases, creating a dedicated knowledge-sharing platform and/or hosting workshops and seminars to share and build success. | X | |
| Undertake risk management and measure impact to reduce possible loss and damage, and increase trust. | X | X |
| Define test standards, methods and quality certificates, using standardisation as a catalyst for innovation. | X | X |
| Use appropriate e-procurement and IT tools to carry out a proper risk assessment to measure impact. | X | X |

Source: Adapted from OECD (2017[27]), *Public Procurement for Innovation: Good Practices and Strategies*, https://dx.doi.org/10.1787/9789264 265820-en.

An adequate public procurement regulatory framework can make a substantial contribution to the development of innovative solutions. For instance, contracting authorities under the EU public procurement directives (EC, n.d.[31]) have the possibility to implement the following procedures:

- **Pre-commercial procurement** (PCP): This can be used by procurers when there are no near-to-the-market solutions yet that meet all of the procurers' requirements and new R&D is needed to get new solutions developed and tested to address the procurement need.
- **Public procurement of innovative solutions** (PPI): This can be used by procurers when challenges of public interest can be addressed by innovative solutions that are nearly or already in small quantity on the market.
- **Innovation partnership**, which allows for the combination of research and procurement.

However, none of these procedures have been used in procurement processes in Bratislava and the Slovak PPA and policies only mention the innovation partnership. In order to provide a more comprehensive and flexible framework for innovation, the PPO could clarify the possibility of using all three procedures in the PPA.

Among its medium-term priorities, in 2019, the city established a Living Lab initiative (Bratislava City Lab) to test products and services in a realistic environment, including piloting new innovative technologies and processes across the city hall and city organisations. This initiative will allow for testing them in the live environment to support innovation and improve the quality and effectiveness of city services. The city already implemented four City Lab pilot projects, including one on implementing parking sensors and sensors for detecting urban heat islands. The pilots are financed by the participating companies, which means that no public procurement activities are involved yet. However, at the implementation phase, the city will need to use procurement processes to procure adequate solutions using a competitive process. To advance its innovation agenda, the city of Bratislava should consider integrating the dedicated innovation procedures mentioned in the PPA in its internal procurement directives and explore the possibility of spurring innovation in procurement operations when possible, even through pilot projects. The PD could also collaborate with the innovation team of the city of Bratislava and use their expertise to promote joint projects.

Furthermore, the working group mentioned in the internal directives to review and discuss the relevant award criteria in procurement operations does not include the innovation team, which the city could consider involving in this working group.

Embedding innovation in public procurement also requires changing the way public procurers are working and raising the awareness of different stakeholders on the key role of procurement in enhancing the uptake of innovation. Traditionally, public procurement tenders are drafted to procure specific goods and services, which implies that a solution has already been chosen. A shift is essential in the way public procurement tenders are drafted to reflect better the challenges faced by the contracting authorities and to open the possibility of accepting new solutions from the market. Different city stakeholders have identified this traditional approach as a key challenge to advance Bratislava's innovation agenda through public procurement and to implement the smart cities agenda. As requiring areas are highly involved in the procurement process, namely through the needs and market analysis but also in the development of technical specifications, the city of Bratislava could consider developing a tailored programme to raise awareness and build capacity on the use of procurement to spur innovation.

Another important field of action could target digital strategies and approaches. Digital transformation is key to enhancing the productivity and efficiency of public administration. The city of Bratislava has identified the digital transformation of city services as a key medium-term priority. This digital transformation includes the development of a digital account for residents, the transformation of city organisations and the modernisation of city services. Furthermore, the COVID-19 pandemic accelerated investments in digital infrastructures and equipment such as mobile phones, laptops and servers. This digital transformation requires several procurement processes (e.g. in terms of IT services, equipment and hardware).

The IT department, which is leading the digital transformation of the city, highlighted vendor lock-in as a challenge. A lock-in situation will usually imply that procurement documents for the next contract related to the ICT system causing the lock-in will contain references to the brand name of that system. According to a European Commission (EC) study, EUR 1.1 billion is lost every year in the public sector due to this issue and its impact on competition (EC, 2013[32]). In 2013, the EC published a guide for the procurement of standards-based ICT, which looks into several areas including the assessment of standards, the need for an ICT strategy, the key role of market engagement, etc. (EC, 2013[33]). Given the important digital transformation that Bratislava is currently undertaking, it could be beneficial to develop an ICT procurement strategy that takes into account different risks including vendor lock-in.

## 2.3. Measuring the effectiveness of public procurement in achieving public procurement outcomes and its contribution to the city strategy

In many OECD countries, public procurement has been used as a strategic tool to achieve different policy objectives, supporting governments in advancing their strategic agenda. This requires having a measurement framework in place to assess progress and achievements. The OECD Recommendation on Public Procurement highlights the need to drive performance improvements through evaluation of the effectiveness of the public procurement system, from individual procurements to the system as a whole, at all levels of government where feasible and appropriate (Box 2.4) (OECD, 2015[2]).

---

**Box 2.4. The evaluation principle of the OECD Recommendation on Public Procurement**

**i) Assess periodically and consistently the results of the procurement process**

Public procurement systems should collect consistent, up-to-date and reliable information and use data on prior procurements, particularly regarding price and overall costs, in structuring new needs assessments, as they provide a valuable source of insight and could guide future procurement decisions.

**ii) Develop indicators to measure performance, effectiveness and savings of the public procurement system** for benchmarking and to support strategic policy making on public procurement.

Source: OECD (2015[2]), *OECD Recommendation of the Council on Public Procurement*, https://www.oecd.org/gov/ethics/OECD-Recommendation-on-Public-Procurement.pdf (accessed on 10 November 2017).

---

The city of Bratislava does not undertake any regular evaluation to assess existing processes and institutions and to identify any functional overlaps, inefficient processes, silo approaches and other causes of waste. However, the update of the public procurement internal directives aims at streamlining the procurement process and enhancing its efficiency.

Monitoring and evaluating procurement systems usually requires developing KPIs. KPIs aim at analysing data based on performance objectives and setting actionable goals for improvement (Oxford College of Procurement and Supply, n.d.[34]). The first step is therefore to set SMART objectives, i.e. Specific, Measurable, Assignable, Realistic and Time-related goals (OECD, 2019[12]).

Regarding the evaluation of individual tenders, the city of Bratislava uses a limited number of KPIs: the average number of bidders per procurement opportunity and savings. However, the environmental department is using KPIs related to GPP, both for their own procurement and for one of the waste management company under its supervision. Despite the limited number of KPIs developed by Bratislava so far, they are supporting the development of targeted procurement strategies, which can be considered a good practice. To allow for a more comprehensive understanding of the system's performance, the city of Bratislava should consider defining a larger set of objectives and outcomes and implement more indicators in line with its strategic objectives and with the legal framework. Table 2.2 provides examples of relevant KPIs that are used by contracting authorities on individual procurement operations and that can be aggregated at the contracting authority level.

### Table 2.2. Example of KPIs to be used by contracting authorities

| Procurement cycle | KPI | Details | At the contracting authority level |
| --- | --- | --- | --- |
| Tendering phase | Savings | • Historical or reference price - final price proposed by the awarded supplier | $= \dfrac{\sum Savings}{\sum Procurement\ expenditures} \times 100$ |
| | Procurement method used | • Open tenders<br>• Restricted procedures<br>• Direct award | $= \dfrac{\sum open\ tenders}{\sum procedures} \times 100$<br><br>$= \dfrac{\sum restricted\ tenders}{\sum procedures} \times 100$<br><br>$= \dfrac{direct\ award}{\sum procedures} \times 100$ |
| | Number of bidders | • Total number of bidders<br>• Total number of qualified bidders | $= \dfrac{\sum bidders}{\sum procedures} \times 100$<br><br>$= \dfrac{\sum qualified\ bidders}{\sum procedures} \times 100$<br><br>$= \dfrac{\sum qualified\ bidders}{\sum CNumber\ of\ bidders} \times 100$ |
| | Use of BPQR criteria | • The use of BPQR criteria in the contract | $= \dfrac{\sum procedures\ using\ BPQR\ criteria}{\sum procedures} \times 100$ |
| | Green procurement | • The inclusion of green elements in tenders (qualification/award criteria, technical specification, contract performance clauses, etc.) | $= \dfrac{\sum Procedures\ with\ green\ elements}{\sum procedures} \times 100$ |
| | Social procurement | • The inclusion of social elements in tenders (qualification/award criteria, technical specification, contract performance clauses, etc.) | $= \sum \dfrac{procedures\ using\ social\ elements}{\sum procedures} \times 100$ |
| | SMEs | • Awarding the contract to SMEs | $= \dfrac{\sum contracts\ awarded\ to\ SMEs}{\sum Contracts} \times 100$ |
| | Innovation | • The use of procurement procedures for innovation<br>• The inclusion of requirement that spurs innovation in the tender documentation | $= \dfrac{\sum innovation\ procurement\ procedures}{\sum procedures} \times 100$<br><br>$= \dfrac{\sum procedures\ with\ innovation\ requirements}{\sum procedures} \times 100$ |

| Procurement cycle | KPI | Details | At the contracting authority level |
|---|---|---|---|
| | Challenges | • Number of challenges<br>• Number of grounded challenges | $=\dfrac{\sum challenges}{\sum procedures}x\,100$<br><br>$=\dfrac{\sum groundes\ challenges}{\sum procedures}x\,100$<br><br>$\dfrac{\sum groundes\ challenges}{\sum challenges}x\,100$ |
| Contract management phase | Delivery on time at the quality required | • Delays in delivery (in number of days)<br>• Compliance with the contract requirement | $=\dfrac{\sum contracts\ with\ delays}{\sum contracts}x\,100$<br><br>$=\dfrac{\sum contracts\ compliant\ with\ the\ requirements}{\sum contracts}x\,100$ |
| | Efficiency tools used | • Procurement volume spent on FAs<br>• Procurement volume spent on DPS<br>• Procurement volume spent on e-auctions | $=\dfrac{\sum procurement\ volume\ spent\ on\ FA}{\sum procurement\ voulme}x\,100$<br><br>$=\dfrac{\sum procurement\ volume\ spent\ on\ DPS}{\sum procuement\ voulme}x\,100$<br><br>$=\dfrac{\sum procurement\ volume\ spent\ on\ e-auctions}{\sum procurement\ voulme}x\,100$ |
| | Litigation | • Litigation on a specific contract | $=\dfrac{\sum litigations}{\sum contracts}x\,100$ |
| | Contracts amendments | • Number of contracts amendments | $=\dfrac{\sum contract\ amendments}{\sum contracts}x\,100$ |
| Conclusion of the contract | Payment deadline | • Delays in payment (in number of days) | $=\dfrac{\sum invoices\ with\ delayed\ payment}{\sum invoice}x\,100$<br><br>= average payment deadlines |

Note: FA: Framework agreement; DPS: Dynamic purchasing system.

Furthermore, according to the zIndex platform that publishes data on the score obtained by different public entities on various public procurement aspects, the city of Bratislava had a score of 75% in 2020 which is relatively good (the third place in the category of large cities behind the city of Prešov (77%) and the city of Poprad (76%) (zIndex, 2020[18])).

In addition to assessing the procurement system from individual procurements to the system as a whole, the city of Bratislava could consider assessing the contribution of public procurement to the strategic agenda of the city. Procurement KPIs should be included in the overall city objectives' framework. For instance, for strategies related to sustainability, the city of Bratislava could include KPIs related to green or social elements in procurement operations. For example, the city of Oslo, Norway, aims to be a green, inclusive and smart city, which has also made it a champion of sustainable procurement. Oslo has been pursuing sustainable procurement actions for many years and has placed a particular focus on reducing greenhouse gas emissions, increasing responsible and circular purchasing, and increasing the share of sustainable food (Procura+ Network, n.d.[35]).

The measurement of relevant KPIs requires implementing an adequate information system with relevant data (OECD, 2019[36]). In the city of Bratislava, some indicators can be measured using data from the e-procurement platforms. However, some of them require an adequate internal information system able to collect multiple procurement data across all departments for several years. Currently, the city of Bratislava is using Microsoft Excel files to gather public procurement data. After deciding on its procurement KPIs, the city of Bratislava could consider designing a more sophisticated internal system able to collect relevant procurement data to measure the desired KPIs.

## 2.4. Reinforcing the capacity and capabilities of the procurement workforce of the city

The capacity and capabilities of the public procurement workforce are pivotal for the effective implementation of public procurement processes and thus for the delivery of public services to citizens. The OECD experience shows that the most prominent weakness in public procurement systems is the workforce's lack of capability (defined as the skills-based ability for an individual, group or organisation to meet obligations and objectives) and lack of capacity (defined as the ability to meet obligations and objectives based on existing administrative, financial, human or infrastructure resources). Challenges for public procurement practitioners include the transition from an ordering function to a strategic one; increasingly complex rules; the multidisciplinary nature of the profession; and the lack of professionalization (OECD, 2019[13]). Such challenges are also shared by the city of Bratislava, which faces a lack of educated and experienced procurement experts.

### 2.4.1. Identifying key competencies for city officials involved in procurement operations

To enhance the capacity and capabilities of the procurement workforce, countries may adopt different approaches, such as recognising public procurement as a specific profession, developing certification frameworks and promoting regular procurement training (OECD, 2019[13]). Based on a 2019 OECD survey, the Slovak Republic does not recognise public procurement as a specific profession. Furthermore, there are no specific entry requirements or certifications to work in the public procurement field. According to the city of Bratislava, procurement officials should preferably have an educational background in law or the economy. In addition, no consistent procurement competencies have been integrated into the job profiles of officials involved in procurement operations. Based on stakeholder mapping, in co-operation with the human resources department, the city could identify key procurement and soft competencies for the different categories of officials involved in procurement operations (see Figure 1.3).

In this regard, Bratislava could be inspired by the ProcurCompEu competency framework developed by the EC. The implementation of this framework is derived from the EC recommendation on the professionalisation of public procurement. The framework includes 30 competencies divided into 6 categories: 3 procurement-specific (i.e. needs assessment, tender documentation, contract management, etc.) and 3 soft competencies (i.e. project management, organisational awareness, stakeholder relationship management, etc.) (Figure 2.7). The EC also provides a self-assessment tool that public procurement professionals and organisations can use to assess their levels of proficiency and organisational maturity in the competencies identified in the competency matrix.

### Figure 2.7. Clusters of competencies identified in the EC ProcurCompEu framework

Source: EC (2020[37]), *European Competency Framework for Public Procurement Professionals*, European Commission.

### 2.4.2. Developing tailored training programmes on procurement processes and mechanisms

The city of Bratislava does not have any mandatory training for officials in charge of procurement activities. In order to enhance their capabilities, the city could consider developing a structured training programme for its procurement officials including a minimum number of training programmes each year. This would be even more relevant given: i) the tendency for increased centralisation and the trend for aggregation of needs within the city and its organisations; and ii) Bratislava's ambition to advance its sustainability agenda.

As described in the previous section, in addition to city officials working in the PD, different officials within the city are confronted with public procurement issues. For instance, subject matter experts working in different departments of the city are in charge of developing technical specifications and are responsible for contract management. No formal and regular training on public procurement is available to those officials.

As mentioned, the city has been working on updating the internal directives on procurement through an inclusive approach. Given the complexity of the Slovak PPA, these directives are key to enhancing the capacity of all officials involved in the procurement process of the city. According to the PD, once the internal directives have been finalised and approved by the mayor, all officials within the city involved in public procurement will receive training on the new directive. Bratislava could consider going beyond the internal directives and provide general training programmes on public procurement covering different topics throughout the procurement cycle to all officials involved in procurement processes.

### 2.4.3. Develop standardised procurement documents

The reinforcement of the capabilities of all officials involved in procurement operations could also be supported by the development of standardised documents and templates (OECD, 2016[38]). In this regard, across the EU and OECD, many national and subnational governments such as Barcelona, Spain, and Edinburgh, United Kingdom, have developed specific procurement templates. When not provided by the upper-level government, local governments can also develop their own templates. For instance, the city of

New Orleans, United States, publishes all procurement forms, templates, policies and procedures on line (Box 2.5).

In 2020, the legal department of the city of Bratislava started to develop standardised documents, such as templates for below-threshold contracts and templates for DPS. The city also developed a list of "must-have provisions" in contracts. Bratislava could enlarge its efforts by developing additional procurement templates and standardised documents such as those related to market analysis, needs analysis, evaluation of tenders, etc. Once developed, they could be integrated into the internal public procurement directives and be published.

---

### Box 2.5. Procurement forms published by the city of New Orleans in the United States

- Tax Clearance Form: Form to receive clearance from delinquencies on city taxes.
- Micro Purchase Professional Services Form: For professional service purchases under USD 3 000.
- Small Purchase Professional Services Form: For professional service purchases under USD 15 000.
- Bid Procurement Authorization Form - Materials and Supplies: Form authorising procurement.
- Bid Procurement Authorization Form - Non-Professional Services: Form authorising procurement.
- Bid Procurement Authorization Form - Public Works: Form authorising procurement.
- Request for Professional Services Solicitation Form: Form authorising solicitation for request for proposals/request for qualifications (RfP/RfQ).
- RfP Template.
- RfQ Template.
- RfP/RfQ Checklist: The RfP/RfQ checklist must be completed prior to submitting the solicitation to the Bureau of Purchasing and a copy of the checklist must be included with the request.
- Invitation to Bid Materials and Services Template.
- Invitation to Bid Public Works and Capital Projects Template.
- Invitation to Quote Intake Form – Movables.
- Form for Invitation to Quote – Process for Movables.
- Invitation to Quote Intake Form – Non-Professional Services.
- Form for Invitation to Quote – Process for Non-Professional Services.
- Vendor Performance Evaluation Form: Form used to report vendor performance.
- Independent Cost Estimate Form (ICE).
- Cost Reasonableness Analysis Template.

Source: City of New Orleans (2021[39]), *Purchasing - Forms, Templates, Policies and Procedures*, https://www.nola.gov/purchasing/forms/ (accessed on 7 April 2021).

## 2.5. Strengthening transparency and risk management of the procurement process to enhance citizens' trust

### 2.5.1. Transparency in procurement spending is key to strengthening citizens' trust

Transparency is key for the well-functioning of the public procurement system, it is also central to promoting good governance in the public sector. It fosters accountability, integrity and ensures access to information while enabling the participation of diverse stakeholders. The OECD Recommendation on Public Procurement calls on "Adherents to ensure an adequate degree of transparency of the public procurement system in all stages of the procurement cycle" (OECD, 2015[2]).

However, transparency is not limited to publishing information and data on public procurement. It should also ensure the availability of information to different stakeholders in a user-friendly format. Like many regulatory frameworks across the globe, the Slovak Republic includes transparency as a key principle of its PPA, together with the principles of equal treatment, non-discrimination of economic operators, proportionality, and economy and effectiveness.

Public procurement data of the city of Bratislava can be found on different sources: the website of the PPO, the e-procurement platform Josefine, the EKS electronic contracting system used by the city to place orders and the website of the city of Bratislava (City of Bratislava, 2020[40]). A dedicated webpage on the website of the city provides a single gateway as it includes the links towards all of these platforms.

The PPO website makes it possible to filter the information for each contracting authority by providing "a contracting authority profile". For each of these profiles, the website provides information such as identification details, the list of tender notices, a list of contracts, etc. However, it is not possible to find the estimated value of contracts.

The e-procurement platform Josefine used by Bratislava does not cover the whole procurement cycle, as it only provides information related to the tendering phase. This platform therefore only includes information on ongoing tenders, such as its identification number, the Common Procurement Vocabulary (CPV) code used, the estimated value of the contract (although this section is rarely filled), the deadline for submitting bids, the type of procedure, the inclusion of lots, etc.

The third platform used by the city of Bratislava is the EKS platform used for below-threshold procurement of common goods and services. However, this platform does not enable specific qualification criteria and other award criteria than the lowest price. The system is anonymous, in the sense that bidders do not know for which contracting authority they are submitting a bid and contracting authorities do not know who the bidders are. This platform makes it possible to award a contract rapidly as bidders have a deadline of three working days to submit their offer. However, according to the city of Bratislava, this system is rarely used because there are issues with the selected suppliers in terms of contract performance, as the awarded supplier is only known after the signature of the contract. Furthermore, the website of the city of Bratislava includes a section on "Budget and management", where it is possible to find the budget approved for 2020-22. This document also provides relevant information to different stakeholders on the strategic orientation of the city in terms of spending areas and amounts. However, the information is provided in portable document format (PDF), which is not user-friendly. For the years 2016-19, an "open data" tool shows the budget expenditures of the city. The table below indicates where the public procurement information on the city of Bratislava is available.

## Table 2.3. Mapping of information availability on public procurement in Bratislava

| | PPO website | E-tendering platform (Josefine) | EKS | City of Bratislava website |
|---|---|---|---|---|
| Procurement plans | | | | |
| Budget availability | | | | X |
| Prior information notice | X | | | |
| Tender notice | X | | X | |
| | X | | | |
| Tender documents | X | X | | |
| Qualification criteria | X | X | X | |
| Evaluation criteria | X | X | | |
| Clarification on bidder's question | X | X | | |
| Award notice | X | | | |
| Evaluation report | X | | | |
| Decisions on appeals | X | | | |
| Real-time orders | | | | |
| Contract amendment | X | | | x |
| Invoices | | | | x |
| Schedules and milestones | | | | |
| Physical progress reports | | | | |
| Financial progress reports | | | | |

Source: Based on data provided by the city of Bratislava.

While all these platforms provide a wealth of information, they do not allow citizens and stakeholders to explore the data in a user-friendly format following the budget cycle. It is difficult to match the budget published on the city website and the related procurement spending. The city of Bratislava is therefore planning to improve the user-friendliness of procurement data. For instance, the city of Montreal, Canada, has implemented the open contracting partnership standard, which enables disclosure of data and documents at all stages of the procurement process by defining a common data mode and provides the public with a large variety of information, which can be filtered by date, procurement volume, authorising body and sector (City of Montreal, 2021[41]). The city of Bratislava could therefore consider providing procurement stakeholders, including citizens, with data on procurement spending in a similar user-friendly format. This data could be filtered by year, procurement category and procurement method. It could also include information on planned data and real spending.

Bratislava does not publish procurement plans, even though these can be considered as a key tool to engage the market by providing visibility on the upcoming needs of the city. In terms of contract performance, citizens do not have access to information such as schedules and milestones of the implementation of procurement processes or physical progress reports. The need to access procurement information holds particularly true for large infrastructure projects impacting the daily life of citizens such as those related to mobility. The city could therefore consider publishing procurement plans and information on the performance of contracts to enhance transparency and citizens' trust.

Furthermore, in the Slovak PPA, the publication of public procurement opportunities depends on procurement thresholds. For above EU threshold, it is mandatory to publish procurement opportunities in the European Journal. For below-threshold, depending on the estimated value, there are two different rules: i) for below-limit contracts (i.e. above EUR 70 000 for goods and services), procurement opportunities should be published in the Slovak Journal; ii) for low-value contracts (below EUR 70 000 for goods and services), there is no obligation to publish. In line with good practices, the city of Bratislava also voluntarily publishes low-value contracts in the Slovak Journal.

### 2.5.2. Integrating public procurement activities in the risk management assessment of cities

Public procurement is a high-risk area due to the financial volumes at stake, the multitude of stakeholders and sectors involved. The nature of the risks affecting the procurement system throughout the procurement cycle ranges from integrity and efficiency to environmental and social risks (OECD-HAICOP, 2019[42]).

Applying risk management frameworks to public procurement activities is crucial to inform procurement decisions and to implement mitigation measures that can support cities in better providing public services and achieving their objectives. The COVID-19 pandemic highlighted important deficiencies in risk management assessments, including in public procurement. Many governments, including local ones, are working towards further embedding risk management in their operations (OECD, forthcoming[10]). In the city of Bratislava, there is no formal risk management assessment on procurement activities to inform procurement strategies. However, risks may be discussed at the individual procurement level when possible.

The internal control department of the city identified several challenges and risks related to public procurement, such as tender fragmentation, lack of compliance with the procurement directives, issues with the estimation of contracts and with the planning. This department developed a risk management strategy, which is used to plan inspections. Bratislava could therefore benefit from putting in place a comprehensive risk management strategy for its procurement operations. Other cities in OECD countries, such as the city of Greater Geelong, Australia, have developed such strategies and integrated them in their procurement policies (City of Greater Geelong, 2020[43]).

Regarding integrity risks, public procurement is one of the government activities that is the most vulnerable to corruption. In addition to the volume of transactions and the financial interests at stake, corruption risks are exacerbated by the complexity of the process, the close interaction between public officials and businesses, and the multitude of stakeholders (OECD, 2016[44]). Integrity breaches have direct and indirect costs, affecting the quantity and quality of public services provided to citizens. Integrity risks can occur throughout the procurement cycle, from the needs assessment to the conclusion of the contract. Specific attention is required at the local level, as citizens have more interactions with government representatives at this level (Schöberlein, n.d.[45]).

In 2020, the Slovak Republic ranked 60th out of 180 countries in the Corruption Perceptions Index (in 2019, it ranked 59th) (Transparency International, 2019[46]; 2020[47]). At the national level, the PPA includes provisions aiming at safeguarding the integrity of the system. For instance, a section is dedicated to conflicts of interests (Section 23) and a code of ethics for economic operators has been developed to preserve the public interest principles of public procurement, and safeguarding competition. This code of ethics also applies to subcontractors and other entities involved in the public procurement process (Public Procurement Office, 2015[48]).

At the local level, the city of Bratislava has developed its own code of ethics for all its employees and is planning to update it by the end of 2021. This code includes targeted provisions for high-risk areas such as public procurement. However, there are currently no initiatives at the city level to enhance integrity in the public procurement system. The city could consider raising the awareness of city officials and external stakeholders including civil society organisations and business representatives about integrity.

# References

City of Bratislava (2020), *Public Procurement in the City of Bratislava*, [40]
https://bratislava.sk/sk/verejne-obstaravanie (accessed on 27 November 2020).

City of Greater Geelong (2020), *Procurement Policy*, [43]
https://www.geelongaustralia.com.au/governance/documents/item/8cc1aebc6d50dd1.aspx
(accessed on 8 April 2021).

City of Montreal (2021), *Montant total des contrats par mois*, Vue sur les contrats, Ville de [41]
Montréal, https://ville.montreal.qc.ca/vuesurlescontrats (accessed on 7 April 2021).

City of New Orleans (2021), *Purchasing - Forms, Templates, Policies and Procedures*, [39]
https://www.nola.gov/purchasing/forms/ (accessed on 7 April 2021).

EBRD (2015), *Are You Ready for eProcurement? Guide to Electronic Procurement Reform*, [4]
European Bank for Reconstruction and Development, https://www.ebrd.com/documents/legal-
reform/guide-to-eprocurement-reform.pdf (accessed on 13 December 2018).

EC (2020), *European Competency Framework for Public Procurement Professionals*, European [37]
Commission.

EC (2020), *Life-cycle Costing*, European Commission. [15]

EC (2016), "City of Barcelona's + Sustainable City Council Programme", *GPP In Practice*, [23]
No. 61, European Commission,
https://ec.europa.eu/environment/gpp/pdf/news_alert/Issue61_Case_Study_124_Sustainable
_City_Barcelona.pdf.

EC (2015), "Public Procurement Guidance for practitionners", European Commission, [14]
http://dx.doi.org/10.2776/578383.

EC (2013), "Against lock-in: Building open ICT systems by making better use of standards in [32]
public", Shaping Europe's digital future, European Commission, https://eur-
lex.europa.eu/legal-content/EN/TXT/?uri=celex%3A52013DC0455 (accessed on
6 April 2021).

EC (2013), "Guide for the procurement of standards-based ICT - Elements of good practice", [33]
European Commission, https://ec.europa.eu/digital-single-market/en/news/guide-
procurement-standards-based-ict-%E2%80%94-elements-good-practice (accessed on
6 April 2021).

EC (n.d.), *Innovation Procurement*, H2020 Online Manual, European Commission, [31]
https://ec.europa.eu/research/participants/docs/h2020-funding-guide/cross-cutting-
issues/innovation-procurement_en.htm (accessed on 31 March 2020).

EU (2014), *Directive 2014/24/EU of the European Parliament and of the Council*, EU Parliament [11]
and Council, Official Journal of the European Union, http://eur-lex.europa.eu/legal-
content/EN/TXT/PDF/?uri=CELEX:32014L0024&from=EN (accessed on 31 January 2018).

NHS (2021), *Dynamic Purchasing Systems - All You Need to Know*, NHS London Procurement [26]
Partnership, https://www.lpp.nhs.uk/for-suppliers/dynamic-purchasing-systems-all-you-need-
to-know/ (accessed on 6 April 2021).

OECD (2021), *Government at a Glance 2021*, OECD Publishing, Paris, https://dx.doi.org/10.1787/1c258f55-en.                                  [19]

OECD (2020), *Broad-based Innovation Policy for All Regions and Cities*, OECD Regional Development Studies, OECD Publishing, Paris, https://dx.doi.org/10.1787/299731d2-en.                                  [20]

OECD (2020), "Cities Policy Responses", http://www.oecd.org/coronavirus/policy-responses/cities-policy-responses-fd1053ff/.                                  [28]

OECD (2020), "Smart cities and inclusive growth: Building on the outcomes of the 1st OECD Roundtable on Smart Cities and Inclusive Growth", OECD, Paris, https://www.oecd.org/cfe/cities/OECD_Policy_Paper_Smart_Cities_and_Inclusive_Growth.pdf.                                  [30]

OECD (2020), *The Circular Economy in Groningen, the Netherlands*, OECD Urban Studies, OECD Publishing, Paris, https://dx.doi.org/10.1787/e53348d4-en.                                  [21]

OECD (2020), *The Circular Economy in Valladolid, Spain*, OECD Urban Studies, OECD Publishing, Paris, https://dx.doi.org/10.1787/95b1d56e-en.                                  [22]

OECD (2020), "The territorial impact of COVID-19: Managing the crisis across levels of government", *Tackling Coronavirus (COVID-19): Contributing to a Global Effort*, OECD Publishing, Paris, https://read.oecd-ilibrary.org/view/?ref=128_128287-5agkkojaaa&title=The-territorial-impact-of-covid-19-managing-the-crisis-across-levels-of-government (accessed on 4 May 2020).                                  [1]

OECD (2020), *Towards a New Vision for Costa Rica's Public Procurement System: Assessment of Key Challenges for the Establishment of an Action Plan*, OECD Publishing, Paris, https://www.oecd.org/costarica/Towards-a-new-vision-for-Costa-Rica%27s-public-procurement-system.pdf (accessed on 22 March 2021).                                  [16]

OECD (2020), "Training on market analysis", OECD, Paris.                                  [8]

OECD (2019), *Productivity in Public Procurement, A Case Study of Finland: Measuring the Efficiency and Effectiveness of Public Procurement*, OECD, Paris, https://www.oecd.org/gov/public-procurement/publications/productivity-public-procurement.pdf (accessed on 31 July 2019).                                  [12]

OECD (2019), *Public Procurement Review of Germany*, OECD, Paris.                                  [9]

OECD (2019), *Reforming Public Procurement: Progress in Implementing the 2015 OECD Recommendation*, OECD Public Governance Reviews, OECD Publishing, Paris, https://doi.org/10.1787/1de41738-en.                                  [13]

OECD (2019), *Revue du système de passation des marchés publics en Algérie: Vers un système efficient, ouvert et inclusif*, Examens de l'OCDE sur la gouvernance publique, OECD Publishing, Paris, https://dx.doi.org/10.1787/49802cd0-fr.                                  [36]

OECD (2019), "Slovak Republic", in *OECD SME and Entrepreneurship Outlook 2019*, OECD Publishing, Paris, https://doi.org/10.1787/53572c0d-en (accessed on 6 April 2021).                                  [25]

OECD (2018), *Enhancing the Use of Competitive Tendering in Costa Rica's Public Procurement System*, OECD, Paris.                                  [17]

OECD (2018), *Mexico's e-Procurement System: Redesigning CompraNet through Stakeholder Engagement*, OECD Public Governance Reviews, OECD Publishing, Paris, https://dx.doi.org/10.1787/9789264287426-en. [5]

OECD (2018), *Second Public Procurement Review of the Mexican Institute of Social Security (IMSS): Reshaping Strategies for Better Healthcare*, OECD Public Governance Reviews, OECD Publishing, Paris, https://dx.doi.org/10.1787/9789264190191-en. [7]

OECD (2018), *SMEs in Public Procurement: Practices and Strategies for Shared Benefits*, OECD Public Governance Reviews, OECD Publishing, Paris, https://doi.org/10.1787/9789264307476-en. [24]

OECD (2017), *Public Procurement for Innovation: Good Practices and Strategies*, OECD Public Governance Reviews, OECD Publishing, Paris, https://dx.doi.org/10.1787/9789264265820-en. [27]

OECD (2017), *Public Procurement in Chile: Policy Options for Efficient and Inclusive Framework Agreements*, OECD Public Governance Reviews, OECD Publishing, Paris, https://dx.doi.org/10.1787/9789264275188-en. [3]

OECD (2016), *Checklist for Supporting the Implementation of the OECD Recommendation of the Council on Public Procurement*, OECD, Paris, http://www.oecd.org/governance/procurement/toolbox/search/checklist-implementation-oecd-recommendation.pdf (accessed on 15 November 2017). [38]

OECD (2016), *Preventing Corruption in Public Procurement*, OECD, Paris, http://www.oecd.org/gov/ethics/Corruption-in-Public-Procurement-Brochure.pdf (accessed on 31 January 2018). [44]

OECD (2015), *OECD Recommendation of the Council on Public Procurement*, OECD, Paris, https://www.oecd.org/gov/ethics/OECD-Recommendation-on-Public-Procurement.pdf (accessed on 10 November 2017). [2]

OECD (forthcoming), "Unlocking the potential of public procurement in cities", OECD Publishing, Paris. [10]

OECD/Bloomberg (2018), *OECD/Bloomberg Survey of Innovation Capacity in Cities 2018*, https://doi.org/10.1787/f10c96e5-en. [29]

OECD-HAICOP (2019), *Stratégie de Management des Risques dans les Marchés Publics en Tunisie*, https://www.oecd.org/gov/public-procurement/publications/strat%C3%A9gie-management-des-risques-march%C3%A9s-publics-tunisie.pdf (accessed on 11 June 2019). [42]

Oxford College of Procurement and Supply (n.d.), *Improving Performance In Procurement Using Key Performance Indicators*, https://www.oxfordcollegeofprocurementandsupply.com/procurement-performance-kpis/ (accessed on 7 April 2021). [34]

Procura+ Network (n.d.), *SPP in Oslo*, https://procuraplus.org/public-authorities/oslo/ (accessed on 7 April 2021). [35]

Proebiz (2021), *The e-Procurement Platform Josefine*, https://josephine.proebiz.com/sk/profile/hlavne-mesto-slovenskej-republiky-bratislava (accessed on 2 June 2021). [6]

Public Procurement Office (2015), *Public Procurement Act 343/2015*, https://www.slov-lex.sk/pravne-predpisy/SK/ZZ/2015/343/20200101 (accessed on 8 April 2021). [48]

Schöberlein, J. (n.d.), "Lessons learned from anti-corruption efforts at municipal and city level", https://www.u4.no/publications/lessons-learned-from-anti-corruption-efforts-at-municipal-and-city-level.pdf (accessed on 19 May 2020). [45]

Transparency International (2020), *Corruption Perceptions Index*, https://www.transparency.org/en/cpi/2020/index/nzl (accessed on 12 April 2021). [47]

Transparency International (2019), *Corruption Perceptions Index*, https://www.transparency.org/en/cpi/2019/index/nzl (accessed on 8 April 2021). [46]

zIndex (2020), *Hlavné mesto SR Bratislava*, https://www.zindex.sk/submitter/287140/period/12/hlavne-mesto-sr-bratislava/2020 (accessed on 1 April 2021). [18]

# 3. Case study: The procurement of street lighting in Bratislava

This chapter puts the spotlight on how Bratislava can use public procurement strategically to improve a concrete example of public service, i.e. street lighting. The first section analyses the role of street lighting in citizens' quality of life and in advancing Bratislava's smart city agenda. It offers an overview of the current street lighting system in Bratislava and points out the need to renew it. The second section delves into how to design a tailored public procurement strategy on street lighting. It does so by providing methodological guidance on the analysis of needs, market engagement and tender design.

Cities across the world are using street lighting solutions to improve public service delivery and solve issues related to public safety, air and water quality, mobility, among others. Technology developments in cities involving street lighting projects are also a key component of smart city initiatives. These initiatives are also intended to ensure that all people have access to services and to improve their quality of life. Street lighting enables the provision of different services ranging from safety to health, by reducing crime and vehicle accidents for example. Switching from traditional lighting operations to intelligent lighting networks can help improve public service delivery by reducing energy consumption, improving public safety and the efficiency of maintenance. However, procuring street lighting systems is a constant challenge for cities, especially as they typically entail large upfront costs. The city of Bratislava is in the process of launching several tenders to procure its new street lighting system. This chapter highlights the role of street lighting in providing better services to citizens and aims at supporting Bratislava in the development of the procurement strategy for its street lighting project.

## 3.1. Street lighting: A key public service for citizens

### 3.1.1. The role of street lighting in the provision of public services to citizens

Street lighting is a key public service for citizens as it improves safety for both pedestrians and vehicles. For example, street lighting helps make streets safer, particularly for women and girls. Gender-balance violence (GBV) against women and girls is a complex phenomenon that exists in many different forms and may be experienced not only within family and intimate relationships but also in public spaces (OECD, 2021[1]). While many policies and programmes are needed towards the eradication of GBV, better street lighting, combined with a wider monitoring system, can be a key step towards preventing sexual violence in the streets. This can have a relevant impact in Bratislava, for example, where women represented 53% of the total population in 2020 (Statistical Office of the Slovak Republic, 2021[2]).

The provision of street lighting enables different public services ranging from safety to health. Not only can the improvement in safety support the health system by helping reduce risks of accidents and crimes, the use of smart sensors, for example, can also help monitor air, chemical and pollen pollution, and release audio warnings for storms and other imminent dangers. Furthermore, street lighting also includes an aesthetic dimension that makes cities more attractive for tourists.

The functioning of a street lighting system requires different components such as:

- Poles, luminaires and light bulbs.
- Smart sensors and contactors.
- Street light cabinets and cables.

The installation of these components requires various engineering services and public works such as excavation. The functioning of the street lighting system also requires regular maintenance and the use of a control and management system (CMS). The CMS is comprised of hardware installed in/on luminaires to provide at least the option to switch on/off the luminaire, set the dimming profile and provide basic data about the luminaires, for example if they are working, failing and need to be replaced or even if the communication with a luminaire was temporarily lost. The CMS also has hardware installed in cabinets to provide an option to switch on/off the whole cabinet and energy measurement on electrical inputs and outputs setting the notifications on fault situations when the expected consumption is not met, for instance. Finally, the CMS usually includes software to provide options to set the switching/dimming profiles, visualisation of measurements, evidence of the failures, scheduling the maintenance plans and public access for failure reporting, among others. Figure 3.1 provides an overview of the key elements of a street lighting system. When cities aim to implement a new street lighting system, they should consider all the components needed during the lifespan of the infrastructure to be able to choose the most efficient solution and to avoid facing interoperability issues.

Figure 3.1. Key components of a street lighting system

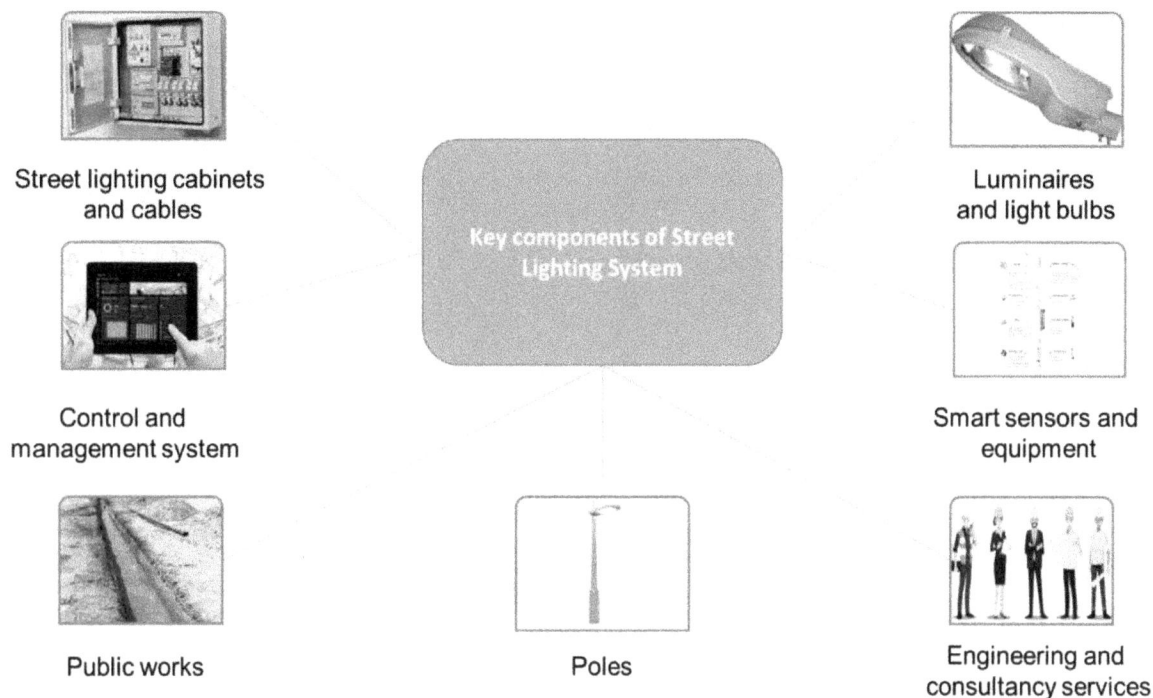

Street lighting cabinets and cables

Control and management system

Public works

Key components of Street Lighting System

Poles

Luminaires and light bulbs

Smart sensors and equipment

Engineering and consultancy services

### 3.1.2. Street lighting to enhance the future of smart cities

Many cities have been investing in street lighting projects to advance their smart city strategies and provide better services for citizens. Through smart street lighting systems, cities aim to improve security, achieve energy efficiency, reduce maintenance costs, ensure better data management and generate revenue. Box 3.1 provides an example of smart sensors and equipment that can be used in street lighting projects. In practice, local authorities have fixed data points that are already pre-powered to act as a base for additional sensors. A smarter street lighting system offers the opportunity to control the output of every luminaire.

---

**Box 3.1. Examples of smart sensors and equipment for smart lighting**

**Smart sensors**

- Monitoring cities' environment.
- Noise sensor.
- Air pollution sensor.
- Weather sensor (including anemometer).
- Brightness sensor.
- Inclination and acceleration sensor.

---

**Video monitoring**

- City security monitoring.
- Picture artificial intelligence recognition data collection.

**Wireless network**

- Wi-Fi hotspots.
- 4G LTE node.
- Future 5G node.

**Light-emitting diode (LED) display**

- Advertising display value-added services.
- Publication of public information.
- Customised display service.

**SOS call**

- location through ambulance centre.
- Emergency relief.

**Charging pile**

- Charging of electric vehicle.
- Electric bicycle.
- Mobile phone/tablet/personal computer.

Source: ZATA (2020[3]), *Smart Street Lighting Sensor*, https://www.zataiot.com/zaq-air-quality-sensor-on-smart-street-lights-all-in-one/#cp1 (accessed on 8 April 2021).

From street lighting projects to the entire integration with Internet of Things (IoT) networks, cities are realising the potential in street lighting systems as a vehicle to advance their smart city agenda (Box 3.2) (OECD, 2020[4]) as well as crime detection and traffic crash prevention. For example, in 2021, the city of Atlanta, United States (US), announced an expansion of 10 000 streetlights in targeted areas as part of the One Atlanta—Light Up the Night crime and traffic crash prevention initiative. The city estimates that crime could decrease by as much as 20% in neighbourhoods through streetlight intervention. The possibility of connecting other devices (e.g. cameras, traffic information boards, sensors, etc.) to this control can also contribute to increasing the safety of residents and visitors to the city (e.g. pedestrians, drivers, cyclists, visitors, etc.).

Cities can use the data available to manage better public services for citizens. Data is available in motion sensors and cameras, for example, and it could be used to map traffic flows and identify the best schedule for maintenance. In addition, smart sensors increase revenue opportunities with add-ons available for different advertising opportunities and Wi-Fi hotspots. However, when adding smart sensors to the street lighting system that may transmit data, cities need to consider data privacy by not collecting data on citizens without their consent. In addition, cities can use the street lighting system to communicate with citizens. For instance, during the COVID-19 pandemic, street lighting systems provided alerts and updates on the COVID-19 situation.

---

### Box 3.2. Examples of street lighting in selected cities

Many cities have been investing in street lighting projects to advance their smart cities strategies:

- In 2020, the city of **Tokyo, Japan**, launched a new street lighting project as part of its smart city strategy to shape safer, more effective and fairer urban development. The project is developed with the NEC Corporation and will be connected to a citywide network. With the new eco-friendly infrastructure, all networked street lights can be centrally managed to save energy and optimise maintenance needs.

- In 2018, the city of **Dijon, France**, established a consortium to develop the first centralised and connected solution for city management of its kind in Europe. The project aims to: reduce costs significantly (e.g. by 65% on the energy bill related to street lighting); upgrade and better manage urban equipment (e.g. street lighting upgrade, planning repair and renewal); better co-ordinate services (road network maintenance and waste collection); and improve public safety (via centralised solutions for crisis management). Some of the technologies provide citizens with a smarter system of street lighting, Wi-Fi, closed-circuit television (CCTV), audio animation and smart traffic management.

- In the city of **Wipperfürth, Germany**, a city-wide intelligent lighting network has been installed and feeds local information to the smartphones of citizens and visitors via Bluetooth. By using a downloadable application, smartphone users can access information about local retailers, special offers, company information, directional aides and smart parking.

- The city of **London** and the **Borough of Barking and Dagenham, United Kingdom (UK)**, is deploying more than 28 000 smart street lights via a platform-as-a-service solution. The platform ensures 100% coverage in the dense urban setting where cellular technology is often unavailable. The deployment of smart lighting will help to achieve energy savings goals, lead to a reduction of operational costs, improve service reliability and function as a platform for future smart applications.

- **Bristol City Council, UK**, has replaced the city's original street lighting with a new energy-efficient solution to substantially reduce operating costs, increase safety and create ideal driving conditions. The city has replaced 20 000 street lights, generating cost savings of GBP 1 million per year.

- In **San Jose** and **Los Angeles, US,** as well as in **Barcelona, Spain**, smart lighting solutions are used to provide mobile broadband connectivity. Light poles can be remotely managed and offer a Wi-Fi hotspot that improves mobile network performance across the cities.

Source: OECD (2020[4]),, "Smart cities and inclusive growth: Building on on the outcomes of the 1st OECD Roundtable on Smart Cities and Inclusive Growth", https://www.oecd.org/cfe/cities/OECD_Policy_Paper_Smart_Cities_and_Inclusive_Growth.pdf; Gelsin, A. (2017[5]), "Multiple benefits of smart street lighting solutions in smart cities", https://hub.beesmart.city/en/solutions/the-multiple-benefits-of-smart-lighting.

However, providing street lighting represents a cost for the local government. Approval processes for funding may be long and require multi-year budgeting practices to secure resources for the implementation of the project. Cities may also need to get funding from different sources and upgrade their procurement practices to ensure value for money when engaging in this sort of project (OECD, 2020[6]). Some municipalities still use outdated and inefficient street lighting facilities, which leads to higher energy consumption and increased maintenance costs. Therefore, life cycle costing (LCC) is becoming an even more relevant topic for street lighting in many cities (see section 3.2.2). Public services can be improved by switching from traditional lighting operations to intelligent lighting networks. Networked LED street lighting systems can help cities reduce the energy use of existing street light systems and reduce operations and maintenance costs. In addition, digital systems can minimise street blockages as remote monitoring allows for faster intervention in case of lighting failures. Furthermore, smart dimming can help manage energy consumption to reduce lighting during low traffic hours or enhance lighting in low-income areas to improve safety. An intelligent energy metering system can improve the accuracy to calculate energy consumption, using varying rates and automatic billing.

Street lighting is also a city's largest consumer of electricity and requires a significant maintenance budget. For municipalities with older, inefficient systems, the European Commission (EC) estimated that street lighting could account for 30-50% of their total electricity consumption. It is also estimated that nearly 80% of all street lighting lamps used by cities are being phased out and some of them are no longer available for purchase. These older systems also have a key environmental impact, potentially associated with greenhouse gas emissions and light pollution. Setting energy efficiency requirements in procurement to reduce maximum levels of mercury permitted in lamps, for example, can help cities reduce their environmental impact (EC, 2015[7]).

### 3.1.3. Snapshot of the street lighting system in place in Bratislava

*An overview of the current street lighting system*

Bratislava's public lighting system was fully modernised and reconstructed between 1996 and 2003. The Modernisation and Reconstruction of Public Lighting project replaced all public lighting luminaires and 12 000 lighting poles, including power lines, with the goal of ensuring sustainable public lighting for 20 years. Since these interventions, new public lighting investments have been implemented only partially. For instance, since 2003, the lighting system has been extended with new sections, especially in areas of new construction. Some lighting points have been removed and part of the original system has been retrofitted. However, there is still a significant part of the original lighting system that dates back to the 1970s, which is far beyond its expected lifespan. As a result, many parts of the lighting system (especially power lines, poles and booms) are outdated and require urgent investments.

According to the city, public lighting in Bratislava consists of approximately 47 000 luminaires that are connected to approximately 800 switching cabinets. High-pressure sodium (HPS) street lights are one of the most common street lights used in Bratislava (accounting for 90% of all luminaires) and are present in large areas, manufacturing sites, roadways, parks and parking areas. Bratislava aims to retrofit its HPS street lights with more efficient and eco-friendly LED lights. This new technology would demand high investments, including in terms of the poles and luminaires that the city will need to procure (see section 3.1.1).

The current situation is challenging in the medium to long term, potentially endangering citizen health, property and safety. The most pressing problems of Bratislava's current public lighting system include: i) the significant increase in the failure rate of low wattage lamps; ii) corrosion of poles; iii) deterioration of the power factor of the public lighting equipment due to the age of the equipment, resulting in penalties for non-compliance with the power factor by the distribution network operator. Furthermore, Bratislava highlighted an alarming increase in the number of fault reports in recent years.

Bratislava's contract on street lighting was scheduled to expire in 2017. However, since then, the city has been renewing the contract with the same supplier on a yearly basis. Recently, the national Public Procurement Office (PPO) imposed a fine of EUR 78 948 on the city of Bratislava related to the first extension of the contract. The PPO claimed that the legal conditions for extending the contract had not been met and that the city's arguments on technical and time reasons did not hold since the municipality did not address the need to procure the street lighting system sufficiently in advance.

In 2018, the city of Bratislava launched a tender to renew its street lighting system but the contract was not awarded. According the different stakeholders, the failure of this tender was due to the lack of clarity and the complexity of the tender specifications, underlining the challenges related to poor planning. The current administration is working on a different approach to procuring the street lighting system, as described in the following section.

*Important investments in the street lighting system are required*

Bratislava is launching a new street lighting project in 2021. The goal is to have public lighting fully covered with smart LEDs within five years (by 2025), with estimated savings of more than 40% on total energy consumption. Compared to its previous approach, the city decided to adopt a new procurement approach: instead of awarding one single contract to an economic operator to operate and maintain the street lighting system, it decided to divide the contract into several investments described in Table 3.1.

### Table 3.1. Investments required for the street lighting project

|  | Estimated cost in EUR |
| --- | --- |
| Public works | 80.25 million |
| Groundworks | 50 million |
| Electrical installation and material | 30 million |
| Engineering activities | 0.25 million |
| Goods | 36.5 million |
| Poles | 10 million |
| Lamps | 25 million |
| Control and management system | 1.5 million |
| Smart solutions | 10 million |

Source: Data provided by the city of Bratislava.

Bratislava has identified the need to renew and/or replace the current infrastructure to enable the use of smart technologies and sensors. The reconstruction of the infrastructure includes the replacement and/or addition of cable lines and the replacement of power supply points and outdated luminaires with new LED light sources. Given the lifespan of the infrastructure and the investment cost, the city decided to divide the project into two phases. The first phase of investment includes the replacement of part of the poles, public works, luminaires and the new CMS. The second part of investment in public lighting in Bratislava involves "infrastructural interventions" that need to be conducted within the next ten years, which includes the replacement of 18 000 lighting poles and 750 km of in-ground cables, which will be outdated and potentially dangerous in the coming years.

However, the street lighting project is still missing a holistic approach, as it requires closer co-ordination among departments at the city level, as well as between the city and the regional and national government. Although in close contact with the PPO at the national level and with the Metropolitan Institute and procurement department at the city level, the energy department of the city of Bratislava has not liaised with some relevant stakeholders, such as the innovation team, the transport department, the environment department, etc. The energy department is identifying potential synergies between the street lighting project and district-level investments but there is yet no integrative tool in place. Considering the different players involved, multi-level governance is key to securing the necessary funding to implement the project and support the adequate planning of procurement activities.

## 3.2. Designing a tailored public procurement strategy on street lighting

### 3.2.1. Translating planned investments into procurement opportunities

The city of Bratislava has started its ambitious project of renewing the street lighting system in place over a ten-year period. It has already procured some street poles and started with a pilot project for the procurement of park luminaires for EUR 0.5 million. It is currently preparing a larger tender on street and park luminaires with an estimated value of EUR 5 million. Bratislava plans to replace 25% of the luminaires in 2022. It also awarded a contract on public works using dynamic purchasing systems (DPS) in 2021. After awarding the larger contract on luminaires, the city will develop the tender documentation on the CMS. Table 3.2 provides an overview of procurement opportunities that will be implemented by Bratislava for the street lighting project.

**Table 3.2. Overview of procurement opportunities to be implemented by Bratislava for the street lighting project**

| Procurement | Expected date for | Procurement | Expected date for |
|---|---|---|---|
| Light poles | December 2020 | 0.064 million | One time purchase (OTP) |
| Park luminaires (pilot) | May 2021 | 0.5 million | OTP |
| Street and park luminaires | December 2021 | 5 million | 4 years |
| Public works (DPS) | May 2021 | 4.2 million | 5 years |
| Control and management system | March 2022 | 13.5 million | OTP + 10 years system providing |
| Public works 2 | To be determined | 75 million | Not available |
| Light poles | To be determined | To be determined | To be determined |

Source: Information provided by the city of Bratislava.

Given the budget constraints and the fact that the city cannot commit to procurement activities in the long term, many procurement activities that are necessary are not yet planned. In fact, multi-year budgeting is only possible in Bratislava with a maximum of 3 years, which is much lower than the lifespan of the street lighting system (approximately 20 years). Therefore, many procurement opportunities cannot be planned and committed to in the long term.

In addition to the elements described in the table above, the city of Bratislava is aiming at procuring further smart equipment, including low power charging stations for e-vehicles (for some poles under a pilot project), traffic monitoring, environmental monitoring, cameras, Wi-Fi and advertising screens. While these components are not part of the street lighting project and related procurement operations, they are included in other projects of the city. Therefore, the street lighting project foresees the provision of electrical and data networks to use these components. A key challenge Bratislava will need to address is related to the interoperability between the different data systems. This challenge should be addressed when developing technical specifications for the different tenders.

### 3.2.2. The key role of market analysis and needs assessment

*For a sound market engagement and analysis*

As described in Section 2.1.2, market analysis has a clear impact on the development of technical specifications and on the performance of the contract. As value for money is the primary objective of public procurement, public buyers have to develop an environment that is conducive to competition by reducing the asymmetry of information with economic operators (OECD, 2017[8]). The Street and Roadway Lighting Market is complex as it is segmented by lighting type (conventional and smart lighting), light source (LEDs, fluorescent lamps, and high-intensity discharge lamps), offering (hardware, software), power (below 50W, between 50-150W, more than 150W), end user (highways, street and roadways), and geography (Mordor Intelligence, 2021[9]). Therefore, a sound market analysis is key to understanding the main players in the market and the capacity of the market to respond to the city's needs and reduce the asymmetry of information. In addition to identifying the main players and the solutions available on the market, this process also helps identify potential interoperability issues, technological changes and vendor lock-in. This holds particularly true given the procurement strategy adopted by the city of Bratislava, moving from one contract for the operation and maintenance of the system to several procurement contracts for different procurement categories.

As mentioned earlier, the city of Bratislava launched a tender in 2018 to renew its street lighting system, which was cancelled. According to some stakeholders, the initial tender developed and published by the city in 2018 was too complicated, triggering many questions from economic operators. This situation highlights the challenges related to the lack of market engagement and understanding of the market environment.

For the procurement of park luminaires, the city launched a tender in 2021 and five economic operators submitted a tender. This pilot exercise helped identify different areas of improvement, including the award criteria set (75% on price and 25% on quality) and the methodology to estimate the value of the contract. Bratislava used the data from the current contract to estimate the unit price of park luminaires. However, the contract price of the awarded contract was approximately three times lower than the estimated ones. While no formal feedback mechanism has been implemented, Bratislava would benefit from such mechanisms to improve its upcoming tender documentation. This is particularly relevant in the framework of pilot projects because they are used to assess project results before implementing a larger-scale project.

To improve suppliers' understanding of the procurement process, receive open feedback on their bids/proposals and identify areas for improvement while encouraging their participation in future tenders, public buyers could be encouraged to organise physical meetings with individual bidders, following a methodology described in Box 3.3.

### Box 3.3. Model format for supplier debriefings

**Opening statement**

- Welcome and introduce the meeting participants.
- Explain the purpose of the debriefing and expectations by procuring authority.
- Outline the parameters of the meeting (i.e. what can/cannot be discussed).
- Outline the structure of the debriefing session.

**Supplier assessment**

- Outline the tendering and evaluation process.
- Describe the evaluation strategy and criteria (e.g. compliance issues, weighting and scoring).
- Outline the size of the field and supplier's relative position (e.g. to the mean score for different criteria).
- Show how supplier scored against main criteria (strengths as well as weaknesses).
- Offer constructive criticism and ways to improve future bids.
- Assess the overall performance, including cost.

**Supplier feedback**

- Provide an opportunity to suppliers to comment or ask questions about the supplier assessment, noting again what can/cannot be discussed.

**Wrap up**

- Enquire about the supplier's views on how the procurement experience can be improved.
- Enquire whether the feedback was useful or if any surprises in the feedback were received.

Source: OECD (2009[10]), *Tool: Guideline and Model Format for Supplier Debriefings*, OECD, Paris.

For large and complex procurement projects, such as the street lighting ones, it is highly recommended to inform the market in advance. In this framework, the publication of a prior information notice (PIN) could have a positive impact on competition. The PIN can be published up to 12 months ahead of the planned launch of the tender and should contain some basic information regarding the goods or services to be purchased (EU, 2014[11]). Bratislava has planned to use it for the procurement of services for the CMS of the street lighting system. However, the city did not plan to publish a PIN for the procurement of luminaires. While participants in the pilot project are aware of the upcoming procurement opportunity, not all players on the market have access to the same level of information. Bratislava could therefore benefit from publishing a PIN as soon as possible for the larger procurement of luminaires. For instance, the city of Paisley, UK, issued a PIN for the procurement of street lighting two months ahead of the publication of the tender (TED, 2018[12]).

While the PIN helps signal upcoming procurement opportunities to the market, the development of the tender documentation, particularly for complex procurements such as street lighting, requires other types of market engagement activities, such as meeting with some key suppliers, open events with suppliers, etc. (see section 2.1.2). An example of an efficient mechanism is to organise direct discussions with the private sector. However, public buyers are often wondering what kind of meetings are more effective: meetings with individual suppliers or a single meeting with different economic operators. Table 3.3 maps the possible benefits and risks of meetings with individual vs. multiple EOs. Given the benefits of both types of meetings and the large investments required, Bratislava could consider undertaking both types of meetings. In any case, public buyers have to adopt an "open agenda", which obliges procurement officials to disclose every meeting they have with the private sector, in order to ensure a level field for competition (OECD, 2009[13]).

**Table 3.3. Benefits and risks of meetings with individual or multiple EOs**

|  | Meetings with individual EOs | Meetings with multiple EOs |
| --- | --- | --- |
| Benefits | • Gathering detailed information on different solutions available in the market<br>• Open discussion | • Same level of information to all suppliers<br>• Reduced risk of information that gives an advantage to one solution |
| Drawbacks/risks | • Provision of information that gives an advantage to one solution<br>• Different levels of knowledge between the first and the last meeting with suppliers | • Collusion<br>• EOs not willing to share information in front of competitors |

*Understanding citizens' needs*

Citizens are the main end users of the street lighting system. As mentioned in section 1.1.4, it is pivotal to understand end users' needs, in particular for large infrastructure projects like the one on street lighting that requires important investments over the next two decades. Citizen feedback and engagement is important for accountability reasons and because procurement and investment choices might have an impact on their daily life.

The city of Bratislava claims it has a good understanding of citizen needs by using the information collected through its application and webpage where any interested party, including citizens, can send specific requests or complaints. While these kinds of tools are important to identify failures of the street lighting system, they are just one aspect of engagement. Box 3.4 provides an overview of the citizen engagement activities for the street light dimming project of Sheffield City Council in the UK. The city of Bratislava could consider reinforcing citizen engagement and the collection of their needs for the street lighting project. This could be done, for instance, by organising meetings with citizens to assess their needs and collect their feedback. This could also be done using digital tools and questionnaires.

---

### Box 3.4. Citizen's engagement for the street light dimming project of Sheffield City Council

**Overview**

In common with many other local authorities and as part of the sustainability agenda, Sheffield City Council is proposing to lower the intensity of street lighting in residential areas across the city. If approved, the changes will support the recently launched Climate Emergency plans, which encourages approaches in support of a lower carbon economy and a reduction in $CO_2$ emissions. The proposals will see street lights switch on responsively at 80% instead of the current 84% before midnight and reduce from 54% to 40% at midnight until 6 am.

The city council wished to emphasise that the proposed level of dimmed lighting levels will still comply with British Standard Specification BS 5489-1 2013, which is the national standard for lighting levels followed by local highway authorities. The city council wants to do this for several reasons:

1.  It will enable the city to reduce greenhouse gas emissions and therefore the contribution to climate change. The city estimates that the proposed reduced lighting across the city will save 380 tonnes of carbon emissions.

2.  It will enable the city to save on the cost of electricity used for street lighting, thereby helping to reduce the financial pressure on already stretched council services.

3.  It will enable the city to reduce light pollution and its likely negative effects on residents' sleep patterns, certain nocturnal animals and plant species. Reduced light pollution will also enable people to derive greater enjoyment from the night sky.

The council plans to trial the reduced lighting levels in three districts of the city – Crosspool, Endcliffe and Meersbrook – from Monday 19 August to Friday 13 September 2019. This will ensure that the city has a sound understanding of the impact of the reduced lighting envisaged before deciding whether or not to go ahead with the proposal. Households in the chosen areas will each receive a letter inviting them to attend an information session in their local library.

South Yorkshire Police are aware of the proposal and the council will continue to work with them and other stakeholders to assess and evaluate the impact on communities. The city will also continue to have the ability to raise local lighting levels where it is sensible to do so in response to local circumstances, emergencies or particular events. The city posted on line a briefing note for citizens.

---

| Goal of the consultation |

**Goal of the consultation**

Public consultation events will take place at Broomhill Library and Highfield Library. These events will provide an opportunity for citizens to provide their feedback.

Source: Sheffield City Council (2019[14]), *Street Light Dimming Trial Survey*, https://sheffield.citizenspace.com/place-business-strategy/street-lighting-consultation/ (accessed on 10 June 2021).

### 3.2.3. Using the right tools for better procurement outcomes

*Setting the right award criteria*

The choice of the award criteria together with the technical specifications developed will have a clear impact on competition and procurement outcomes. As mentioned in section 2.1.4, public contracts can be awarded using different methodologies. Given the complexity of the procurement of street lighting components, in particular for the luminaires, it is recommended to use the most economically advantageous tender (MEAT) criteria, the LCC approach (or total cost of ownership) or a combination of both.

Many cities have used the LCC approach to motivate their decision to move to LED lamps instead of HPS lamps (Box 3.5). While the unit price of LED lamps is higher than the price of HPS, the energy cost associated with each type of technology makes LED technology the more affordable option. That is why the city of Bratislava decided to replace HPS with LED luminaires. According to estimates by Bratislava, the replacement of LED lights will result in energy savings of more than 40% (8 000 MWh per year). In financial terms, at current electricity prices, this would represent savings of approximately EUR 1.2 million per year for Bratislava. Another benefit of using LED technology is the possibility of ensuring power supply at all times. Currently, the power supply infrastructure works primarily at night. It is critical to have a power supply also during the day if Bratislava wishes to integrate smart city sensors.

---

#### Box 3.5. LCC comparisons in US cities

A number of LCC comparisons have been carried out in US cities and towns, where LED uptake for road lighting installations began. Some are briefly described below:

- **Portland**, Oregon, invested USD 18.5 million in replacing 45 000 HPS light points with LED for 50% lower energy consumption — leading to savings of USD 1.5 million per year in reduced energy and maintenance costs. That equates to a payback period of eight years when discount rates are factored in.
- **Los Angeles**, California, invested USD 57 million in replacing 140 000 HPS light points with LED and the energy savings were initially expected to be around 40% but advances in LED technology ahead of the project resulted in greater savings. Together with USD 7.5 million savings in electricity costs, the total annual savings of USD 10 million should result in a payback period of 5 to 6 years. However, the study urged caution in procuring LED solutions, when it was found that only 84 of 244 LED units met the quality specifications set out by the Bureau of Street Lighting website.
- **Charlotte County**, Florida, considered the costs in 2016 of changing their 2 145 light points from HPS to LED lighting. Their existing maintenance costs were assumed to be between USD 28 and USD 55 per light point, depending on the type. The power cost of an HPS light was around USD 12 per month and an LED light was estimated to be USD 6 per month (a 50%

---

reduction). Current energy and maintenance costs (for HPS) are USD 310 000 and USD 80 000 respectively. They concluded that costs for HPS and LED were similar over a 20-year period, but that falling LED costs would soon make it the more economical option.

- In **Phoenix**, Arizona, the conversion of almost 95 000 HPS light points to LED was considered in 2013. Over a period of 10 years, they considered HPS and LED with the following characteristics: energy cost per light per year (HPS: USD 72.36; LED: USD 32.88); fixture cost (HPS: USD 250; LED: USD 475); fixture installation (HPS: USD 29; LED: USD 29); and lamp life (HPS: 20 000 hours; LED: 50 000 hours). In conclusion, they found that LED was around 20% cheaper over a period of 10 years. Applied to the city of Phoenix, this equated to around USD 5 million per year once the whole system was converted. For a USD 1 million investment in LED, a 9-year simple payback period was calculated.

Source: EC (2019[15]), *EU Green Public Procurement Criteria for Road Lighting and Traffic Signals*, https://ec.europa.eu/environment/gpp/pdf/toolkit/181210_EU_GPP_criteria_road_lighting.pdf.

However, in addition to the choice of the technology used, different parameters need to be considered to assess the real cost for the city, including the unit price of each luminaire, energy costs and maintenance/operation costs.

Even when using the same technology, the quality of the equipment might entail different costs that need to be assessed. However, according to the city of Bratislava, many costs such as maintenance cannot be calculated, as these depend on different parameters that cannot be known in advance (e.g. electricity price, frequency of maintenance, etc.). These challenges limit the possibility to use the LCC approach to compare different bids.

In addition to cost elements, other award criteria can be used, such as the quality (including lighting quality and design) and the warranty and availability of spare parts. To strengthen the sustainability approach, a criterion could also be added to the design for recycling. Box 3.6 provides two examples of award criteria and their weighting with and without a total cost of ownership approach, from the PremiumLight-Pro Consortium project funded by the EC. In its pilot project, Bratislava used MEAT criteria, allocating 75% of the weight to price and 25% to quality. The 25% quality is divided into 5% on technical specifications above the minimum standards, 10% on the annual energy consumption indicator (AECI) and 10% on the power density indicator (PDI). For the larger tender on park and street luminaires, Bratislava could consider using a LCC approach or total cost of ownership, using criteria in relation to the warranty and design for recycling. Bratislava could also consider increasing the weight of the qualitative criteria and other non-price criteria.

## Box 3.6. Weighting and award criteria for street lighting projects

For the assessment of the award criteria, a weighting approach is required. For projects where a robust total cost of ownership (TCO) approach can be applied, main aspects including operation and maintenance are already covered and only a few additional parameters like quality, design, warranty and end-of-life aspects are to be added. So, for example, energy consumption and maintenance aspects are already covered in the electricity and maintenance costs and double counting has to be avoided. Consequently, TCO has a large part of the total weight. The weighting of criteria typically has to be adapted to local needs and requirements. Thus, the approach recommended here is just one possible option.

### Table 3.4. Weighting of award criteria for projects including TCO

| Award criteria | | Weighting (%) |
|---|---|---|
| Cost criteria based on TCO | | 50 |
| TCO | Investment costs | 15 |
| | Electricity costs | 20 |
| | Maintenance costs | 15 |
| Quality and design criteria | | 30 |
| Lighting quality | | 20 |
| Design | | 10 |
| Warranty, design for recycling | | 20 |
| Warranty | | 10 |
| Availability of spare parts, design for recycling | | 10 |
| **Total** | | **100** |

### Table 3.5. Weighting of award criteria for projects without TCO

| Award criteria | Weighting (%) |
|---|---|
| Cost criteria | 25 |
| Quality and design criteria | 35 |
| Lighting quality | 25 |
| Design | 10 |
| Energy criteria | 20 |
| Annual energy consumption indicator (AECI) or power density indicator (PDI) or component efficiency | 20 |
| Operation, maintenance and end-of-life criteria | 20 |
| Ease of maintenance, repair | 10 |
| Warranty, availability of spare parts | 10 |
| **Total** | **100** |

Source: PremiumLight-Pro Consortium (2017[16]), "Procurement criteria for LED street lighting".

*Developing technical specifications taking into account technological developments and environmental considerations*

The street lighting area is relatively complex, as it requires technical, legal and financial expertise to choose the best solution. Therefore, when developing technical specifications, it is recommended to use a functional approach. Compared to descriptive technical specifications, designing functional requirements encourages the market to be more innovative, as it gives the suppliers the flexibility to develop a wide range of solutions that respond to a specific need. This method also allows for fair competition between suppliers, therefore providing the public buyers with the best benefit (EC, 2018[17]). Given the rapidly evolving technologies in street lighting, tender documentation should provide enough flexibility to integrate potential changes. For instance, the luminaire efficacy of LED-based lighting is evolving every year and this needs to be reflected in tender documentation (EC, 2018[18]). This challenge holds particularly true when using framework agreements with a duration of four years.

Furthermore, tender specifications for street lighting poles should take into account the possibility of integrating smart sensors and other equipment such as charging stations for electric vehicles and advertisements. According to the city of Bratislava, these elements have been taken into account in the tender launched in 2020.

In addition to technological changes, tender specifications should also consider environmental externalities related to the life cycle of the technology. Figure 3.2 describes the main environmental impacts during the road lighting life cycle and potential approaches to mitigate them in the tender specifications. Many of these approaches have been implemented by Bratislava, such as the proportion of blue light and the upward light output ratio.

## Figure 3.2. Key environmental impacts of road lighting and potential mitigation measures in tender specifications

| Key environmental impacts during road lighting life cycle | Proposed EU GPP road lighting approach |
| --- | --- |
| • $CO_2$ and other greenhouse gas emissions as a result of electricity consumption in the use of road lighting.<br>• Emission of acidifying gases as a result of electricity consumption in the use of road lighting.<br>• Loss of star visibility caused by upward light output from unshielded luminaires and reflection from the ground.<br>• Disruption of nocturnal species' behaviour with potential adverse effects on biodiversity, especially with blue light.<br>• Poor resource efficiency in cases where products or components need to be replaced before the end of their stated lifetime due to, for instance use of lower quality (and cheaper) LED chips and difficulties with repair or to poor installation | • Procure luminaires, lamps or light sources that exceed minimum luminaire efficacies.<br>• Encourage the use of dimming and metering to ensure that energy consumption of a particular lighting installation can be optimised and monitored in real time.<br>• Require that all luminaires have 0.0% upward light output ratio and, at comprehensive level, to ensure that 97% of all light falls within a downward angle of 75.5° to the vertical for the reduction of obtrusive light and glare.<br>• Encourage obligatory dimming in areas of concern and to set limits on the proportion of blue light (G-index) in lamp/luminaire output.<br>• Procure durable and fit-for-use road lighting equipment that is repairable and covered by a warranty or extended warranty.<br>• Set minimum requirements for the person responsible for signing off the lighting installation. |

Note: The order of the impact does not necessarily reflect their magnitude.
Source: EC (2018[18]), *EU GPP Criteria for Road Lighting and Traffic Signals*, http://ec.europa.eu/environment/gpp/buying_handbook_en.htm (accessed on 14 June 2021).

### *Using the adequate efficiency tools*

Given the procurement strategy that Bratislava adopted for its street lighting project, the lifespan of the infrastructure and its key role for the provision of public services of citizens, Bratislava could leverage the efficiency tools available in the Slovak Public Procurement Act (PPA) such as DPS and framework agreements. In fact, Bratislava has already used them in some procurement tenders related to the street lighting project. For instance, the city used a DPS for a tender on public works and a framework agreement for a pilot on park lamps but could expand their use.

In general, the decision to use a DPS or a framework agreement depends mainly on the subject matter of the contract. As mentioned in section 2.1.3, the DPS can be used for purchases that are generally available on the market. In addition, a framework agreement has a maximum duration of four years, while there is no time limit for the duration of a DPS given that it is open to EOs throughout its validity. Considering the lifespan of the street lighting project, the DPS could be an adequate efficiency tool for purchases available on the market. Furthermore, the DPS provides the possibility to update the technical specifications considering new developments. In the framework agreement, the technical specification will be constant unless specifically handled in the agreement (EC, forthcoming[19]). One of the reasons why the city did not use a DPS for the pilot project on park lamps is the issue of uniformity. This issue could have been addressed in the technical specifications of the DPS. Bratislava could therefore consider further exploring the benefits of DPS in the framework of the street lighting project.

# References

EC (2019), *EU Green Public Procurement Criteria for Road Lighting and Traffic Signals*, European Commission, https://ec.europa.eu/environment/gpp/pdf/toolkit/181210_EU_GPP_criteria_road_lighting.pdf. [15]

EC (2018), *EU GPP Criteria for Road Lighting and Traffic Signals*, European Commission, http://ec.europa.eu/environment/gpp/buying_handbook_en.htm (accessed on 14 June 2021). [18]

EC (2018), *Guidance on Innovation Procurement - Commission Notice*, European Commission. [17]

EC (2015), *Street Lighting Refurbishment with Energy Performance Contracting Guide*, European Commission, https://e3p.jrc.ec.europa.eu/publications/streetlight-epc-guide. [7]

EC (forthcoming), *Dynamic Purchasing Systems: A Guideline on the Use of DPS*, European Commission. [19]

EU (2014), *Directive 2014/24/EU of the European Parliament and of the Council*, Official Journal of the European Union, http://eur-lex.europa.eu/legal-content/EN/TXT/PDF/?uri=CELEX:32014L0024&from=EN (accessed on 31 January 2018). [11]

Gelsin, A. (2017), "Multiple benefits of smart street lighting solutions in smart cities", https://hub.beesmart.city/en/solutions/the-multiple-benefits-of-smart-lighting. [5]

Mordor Intelligence (2021), *Street and Roadway Lighting Market - Growth, Trends, COVID-19 Impact, and Forecasts (2021-2026)*, https://www.mordorintelligence.com/industry-reports/street-and-roadway-lighting-market (accessed on 8 April 2021). [9]

OECD (2021), *Strengthening governance and survivor/victim-centred approaches to eliminating gender-based violence*, https://www.oecd.org/mcm/Strengthening%20governance%20and%20survivor-victim-centric%20approaches.pdf. [1]

OECD (2020), *Leveraging Digital Technology and Data for Human-centric Smart Cities: The Case of Smart Mobility*, OECD, Paris, https://www.itf-oecd.org/sites/default/files/docs/data-human-centric-cities-mobility-g20.pdf. [6]

OECD (2020), "Smart cities and inclusive growth: Building on on the outcomes of the 1st OECD Roundtable on Smart Cities and Inclusive Growth", OECD, Paris, https://www.oecd.org/cfe/cities/OECD_Policy_Paper_Smart_Cities_and_Inclusive_Growth.pdf. [4]

OECD (2017), *Public Procurement in Chile: Policy Options for Efficient and Inclusive Framework Agreements*, OECD Public Governance Reviews, OECD Publishing, Paris, https://dx.doi.org/10.1787/9789264275188-en. [8]

OECD (2009), *OECD Principles for Integrity in Public Procurement*, OECD, Paris, https://www.oecd.org/gov/ethics/48994520.pdf (accessed on 9 June 2021). [13]

OECD (2009), *Tool: Guideline and Model Format for Supplier Debriefings*, OECD, Paris. [10]

PremiumLight-Pro Consortium (2017), "Procurement criteria for LED street lighting". [16]

Sheffield City Council (2019), *Street Light Dimming Trial Survey*, [14]
https://sheffield.citizenspace.com/place-business-strategy/street-lighting-consultation/
(accessed on 10 June 2021).

Statistical Office of the Slovak Republic (2021), "DATAcube", [2]
https://slovak.statistics.sk/wps/portal/ext/themes/demography/population/indicators/!ut/p/z1/tV
FNc5swEP0tOXAUWhCfueFMx3Ybd-p0EhtdOhIIUA0SQYqp--
sj0l4607STQ3TanX3a9_Y9TPERU8XOsmVWasV615c0-bZPt9lqFRSQrR5C2Kaf74JP-
_16m4f4AVNMK2VH2-FSc8M6ZE4eGOs2VKjSygplPbBiuH.

TED (2018), *Prior Information Notice*, Tenders Electronic Daily, European Union, [12]
https://ted.europa.eu/udl?uri=TED:NOTICE:4558-2018:TEXT:EN:HTML (accessed on
9 June 2021).

ZATA (2020), *Smart Street Lighting Sensor*, https://www.zataiot.com/zaq-air-quality-sensor-on- [3]
smart-street-lights-all-in-one/#cp1 (accessed on 8 April 2021).